ULTIMATE HANDBOOK

ULTIMATE PRAYER HANDBOOK

HEALTH. MONEY. POWER.

DR. JOHN KING HILL &
DR. EVETTE YOUNG

Harvesters
New York, USA

www.johnkinghillministries.com

USA

866.978.9324

This book and all other Harvesters Publisher ™ books are available at Christian bookstores and distributors worldwide.

To order products, or for any other correspondence:

Email: media@ johnkinghillministries.com

Or reach us on the Internet: www.johnkinghillministries.com

ISBN 13: 978-1-0878-3690-4

ISBN 13 E-BOOK: 978-1-0878-3691-1

For Worldwide Distribution, Printed in the U.S.A.

Dedication

This Book is dedicated to God the Father, Son and the Holy Spirit.

Acknowledgments

Special thanks to:

My wife, Prophetess (Dr.) Evette Young and my daughter Anointed Evelyn-Divine, who have supported, comforted, and assisted me through the process of making this work a reality.

Pastor Benny Hinn (Benny Hinn Ministries, Irving, Texas), who is my spiritual father and mentor;

My Bishop, Pastor Rod Parsley, World Harvest Church, Columbus, Ohio;

My Beloved Family, Apostle Charles Ndifon and Pastor Donna Ndifon, Christ Love Ministries International, Rhode Island USA;

Bishop R.C. & Lisa Blake, New Home Fellowship, New Orleans, Louisiana, USA;

Apostle Carlos Luis and Evelyn Vargas, Freeport Bible Center, Freeport, NY: you are a very dear brother and family to me;

My dear brother, Pastor Victor Hickson, Full Deliverance Baptist Church, Miami, Florida USA;

Prophetess Beatrice Tchoutouo, MD, who never ceases to cheer me up;

Nathan Barnes, PhD, for his editorial contributions.

May His grace abound unto you!

Contents

Preface

The end-times represent the threshold that ultimate — desperate and destitute prayers will be offered with extraordinary weight of God in the earth realm. As the dimensions of all different realms are opened to expose the hidden trenches of the enemies, volleys of prayers will erupt to target the strongholds with demolishing authority and power of the LORD God.

Strongholds are not dismantled by arm-wrestle: there are mighty weapons that deal with mighty powers and dynamic prayers will alter the balance of power in the end-times. The consummation of the glory of the LORD God, the glory of the world — satan's glory, the self-glory and the glory of men will leave no stone unturned! The earth will see great chaos and great revelation, and the human race will dare it all. The olden days experience will call for the men and women of the modern day with the stamina of the olden days to rise up for the occasion. Some will defy the restraints of the natural laws and step into the hidden realms of God.

Dangerous time begs for dangerous prayers! The blazing heat has been rising up — men and women of great sacrifices are being chosen and elected to enter their spiritual positions with Christ in God. Today's everyday events are not what the earth has seen before and neither will see the likes thereafter. All records will be broken and all titles will be exhausted. The appetites of many will be awakened and prayers that are beyond the human concepts and passions will be offered on the altars of the martyred living testimonies.

Death and resurrection as well as ascension and revelation are all parts of the great end-times supernatural transformation — to fulfill the order of the new creation realty. Ultimate prayers are not born in the earth realm; therefore, those who will find the secrets of the end-times great move of the LORD God will sell everything to buy into the treasures. The end-times altars of sacrifices are spiritual — so the baptism of water, baptism of the Holy Spirit and the baptism of fire are all simulation of death until the baptism of death to bring in the martyrs. You must lose yourself to lose the world, and you must lose the world to disappear from the Kingdom of satan's rulership powers.

To escape from the domain of rulership, you must alter your personality, you must take on a different form, look and appearance. You must experience real spiritual change and transformation, which is how earthly biological and genealogical lineages are cut off. Ultimate prayers come with ultimate price, so let us pray!

In His Love,

Apostle (Dr.) John King Hill.

PART ONE

Dynamic Healing Prayer

Father, in the name of Jesus:

Isaiah Chapter 53:7 declares that by His stripes we were healed.

Father, I pray now for the unusual release of your great healing power over the lives of your people wherever this prayer contact material is played or listened to.

I pray that every knee – of all manner of sicknesses and diseases will bow down as your people receive their healing in Jesus name.

Father, let your healing power descend exponentially from your throne of grace and impact the masses through this prayer contact material like the stirring of the pool of Bethesda by the angel of the LORD in John Chapter 5:1-4.

Let your tsunami power like a mighty rushing waves of energy begin to heal all manner of sicknesses and diseases everywhere in Jesus name.

I speak to the life supports systems or breathing apparatus of sicknesses and diseases to fail now, and every root of sicknesses and diseases to be plucked out and be uprooted.

I speak to every sickness and disease to begin to withdraw from their assignments or operations.

I speak to the cells of sicknesses and diseases to suffocate and die now – wither from your foundations and dry up – begin to vanish and disappear from the bodies of the people now: from the privacy of their homes, their businesses, inside their cars, in the airplanes, restaurants or wherever they may be.

I speak to cancers to depart now: throat cancer, brain cancer, stomach cancer, breast cancer, prostate cancer and all other cancer strains – I speak to all cancer cells to be electrocuted by the light energy of the power of God Almighty in Jesus name.

I speak to tumors to melt away now

I speak to sugar diabetes to go now

I speak to viruses to flee

I speak to kidney problems: kidney failure, kidney stone, kidney infections go now

I speak to bone diseases to go

I speak to skin diseases to go

I speak to all manner of infections to begin to disappear

Deafness be loosed now in Jesus name

Dumb mouth begins to speak now

I command paralysis or cerebral palsy to be healed now

I command blind eyes to receive their sights now

I command dysfunctional ligaments to be restored now

I command damaged organs to be restored now

I command birth defects to be healed now

I command mental illnesses, schizophrenia, and mental disorders caused by spiritual and physical traumas or otherwise to be restored now

I command liver diseases to go now

I command heart diseases to go in Jesus name

I call for eating disorder -- bulimia to go now

I call for nerve diseases to go now

I call for spinal conditions to re-align now

I call for all manner of disorders to go now

I call for degenerative diseases to go now

I call for bleeding conditions to stop now

I call for depression to go now

I order every power of sickness and disease to be broken in Jesus name

I order arthritis to vacate now

I order all sexually transmitted and sexually contracted sicknesses and diseases to go now

I order demonically inflicted sicknesses and diseases to go now

I order asthma reactions to cease and decease now

I order allergy infirmities to go now

I order broken hearts to be healed now

I order demonically implanted devices and objects in people's bodies to be rooted out now

Every pain, every sorrow and every grief go now

Every negative blood pressure goes now

Every abnormal breathing or respiratory conditions to be made normal now

Every sleep disorder, insomnia or other sleep deprivation be loosed now

Every sickness and disease existing as a result of warlocks and witchcraft attacks, spells, hex and curses be broken in Jesus name

Every sickness and disease caused by spiritual and physical poisons be healed now

Every migraine disorder be healed now

Every digestive complication goes now

Every blotting of the body goes now

Every blood disease goes now: I call for the transfusion of the blood of Jesus into your body to clear up and alkaline your blood system – be healed now in Jesus name

Every eye condition: cataracts, glaucoma, blurriness and other eye infections, sickness or disease go now

Every irregularity, abnormality, internal or external damages, wounds and injuries be restored now in Jesus name

Wounds of oppression be healed now

Broken bones be formed now

Missing body parts be created now

Deformed bodies be made whole now

Abnormal body odors caused by spiritual pollutions, internal and external decays or induced by demonic powers be reversed now in Jesus name

Wombs that cannot bear children open now

Repeated miscarriages and re-occurring still-births experiences stop right now

I reset your pregnancy cycles and I speak life and preservation over your babies inside the wombs now in Jesus name

I speak to those who are near death or terrorized by the power of death to be loosed now

I command the sting of the fear of death to go and the oppressive wound of death to heal now

The Bible said that the power of life and death is in the power of my tongue

I speak life and not death

I speak restoration

I speak wholeness

I speak completion

I speak perfection

I declare my healing

I declare I am now free

In Jesus name!

NEW TESTAMENT HEALING SCRIPTURES

And he went throughout all Galilee, teaching in their synagogues and proclaiming the gospel of the kingdom and healing every disease and every affliction among the people (Matthew 4:23).

And He called to Him His twelve disciples and gave them authority over unclean spirits, to cast them out, and to heal every disease and every affliction (Matthew 10:1).

Heal the sick, raise the dead, cleanse those who have leprosy, drive out demons. Freely you have received; freely give (Matthew 10:8).

It is not the healthy who need a doctor, but the sick. I have not come to call the righteous, but sinners (Mark 2:17).

He [Jesus] said to her, Daughter, your faith has healed you. Go in peace and be freed from your suffering (Mark 5:34).

And the power of the Lord was with him to heal (Luke 5:17).

Heal the sick in it and say to them, 'The kingdom of God has come near to you (Luke 10:9).

And He laid His hands on her, and immediately she was made straight, and she glorified God (Luke 13:13).

But they remained silent. Then He took him and healed him and sent him away (Luke 14:4).

He has blinded their eyes and hardened their heart, lest they see with their eyes, and understand with their heart, and turn, and I would heal them (John 12:40).

While you stretch out your hand to heal, and signs and wonders are performed through the name of your holy servant Jesus (Acts 4:30).

And Peter said to him, Aeneas, Jesus Christ heals you; rise and make your bed. And immediately he rose (Acts 9:34).

How God anointed Jesus of Nazareth with the Holy Spirit and with power. He went about doing good and healing all who were oppressed by the devil, for God was with him (Acts 10:38).

Our bodies are buried in brokenness, but they will be raised in glory. They are buried in weakness, but they will be raised in strength (1 Corinthians 15:43).

Is anyone among you sick? Let him call for the elders of the church, and let them pray over him, anointing him with oil in the name of the Lord. And the prayer of faith will save the one who is sick, and the Lord will raise him up (James 5:14-15).

Therefore, confess your sins to one another and pray for one another, that you may be healed. The effectual fervent prayer of a righteous man availeth much (James 5:16).

He personally bore our sins in His [own] body on the tree [as on an altar and offered Himself on it], that we might die (cease to exist) to sin and live to righteousness. By His wounds you have been healed (1 Peter 2:24).

Dear friend, I pray that you may enjoy good health and that all may go well with you, even as your soul is getting along well (3 John 1:2).

CASES WHERE JESUS HEALED PEOPLE

Jesus went throughout Galilee, teaching in their synagogues, proclaiming the good news of the kingdom, and healing every disease and sickness among the people. News about him spread all over Syria, and people brought to him all who were ill with various diseases, those suffering severe pain, the demon-possessed, those having seizures, and the paralyzed; and he healed them (Matthew 4:23-24).

Jesus went through all the towns and villages, teaching in their synagogues, proclaiming the good news of the kingdom and healing every disease and sickness (Matthew 9:35).

Jesus called his twelve disciples to him and gave them authority to drive out impure spirits and to heal every disease and sickness...Heal the sick, raise the dead, cleanse those who have leprosy, drive out demons. Freely you have received; freely give (Matthew 10:1-8).

As soon as they left the synagogue, they went with James and John to the home of Simon and Andrew. Simon's mother-in-law was in bed with a fever, and they immediately told Jesus about her. So he went to her, took her hand and helped her up. The fever left her and she began to wait on them. That evening after sunset the people brought to Jesus all the sick and demon-possessed. The whole town gathered at the door, and Jesus healed many who had various diseases. He also drove out many demons, but he would not let the demons speak because they knew who he was (Mark 1:29-34).

On hearing this, Jesus said to them, It is not the healthy

who need a doctor, but the sick. I have not come to call the righteous, but sinners (Mark 2:17).

He said to her, Daughter, your faith has healed you. Go in peace and be freed from your suffering (Mark 5:34).

One day Jesus was teaching, and Pharisees and teachers of the law were sitting there. They had come from every village of Galilee and from Judea and Jerusalem. And the power of the Lord was with Jesus to heal the sick. Some men came carrying a paralyzed man on a mat and tried to take him into the house to lay him before Jesus. When they could not find a way to do this because of the crowd, they went up on the roof and lowered him on his mat through the tiles into the middle of the crowd, right in front of Jesus. When Jesus saw their faith, he said, Friend, your sins are forgiven. The Pharisees and the teachers of the law began thinking to themselves, Who is this fellow who speaks blasphemy? Who can forgive sins but God alone? Jesus knew what they were thinking and asked, Why are you thinking these things in your hearts? Which is easier: to say, Your sins are forgiven, or to say, Get up and walk? But I want you to know that the Son of Man has authority on earth to forgive sins. So he said to the paralyzed man, I tell you, get up, take your mat and go home. Immediately he stood up in front of them, took what he had been lying on and went home praising God. Everyone was amazed and gave praise to God. They were filled with awe and said, We have seen remarkable things today (Luke 5:17-24).

While Jesus was still speaking, someone came from the house of Jairus, the synagogue leader. Your daughter is dead, he said. Don't bother the teacher anymore. Hearing this, Jesus said to Jairus, Don't be afraid; just believe, and she will be healed. When he arrived at the house of Jairus, he did not let anyone go in with him except Peter, John and James, and the child's father and mother.

Meanwhile, all the people were wailing and mourning for her. Stop wailing, Jesus said. She is not dead but asleep. They laughed at him, knowing that she was dead. But he took her by the hand and said, My child, get up! Her spirit returned, and at once she stood up. Then Jesus told them to give her something to eat. Her parents were astonished, but he ordered them not to tell anyone what had happened (Luke 8:49-56).

You know what has happened throughout the province of Judea, beginning in Galilee after the baptism that John preached - how God anointed Jesus of Nazareth with the Holy Spirit and power, and how he went around doing good and healing all who were under the power of the devil, because God was with him (Acts 10:37-38).

As he was going into a village, ten men who had leprosy met him. They stood at a distance and called out in a loud voice, Jesus, Master, have pity on us! When he saw them, he said, Go, show yourselves to the priests. And as they went, they were cleansed. One of them, when he saw he was healed, came back, praising God in a loud voice. He threw himself at Jesus' feet and thanked him—and he was a Samaritan. Jesus asked, Were not all ten cleansed? Where are the other nine? Has no one returned to give praise to God except this foreigner? Then he said to him, Rise and go; your faith has made you well (Luke 12:17-19).

And a woman was there who had been crippled by a spirit for eighteen years. She was bent over and could not straighten up at all. When Jesus saw her, he called her forward and said to her, Woman, you are set free from your infirmity. Then he put his hands on her, and imme-diately she straightened up and praised God (Luke 13:11-

13).

One Sabbath, when Jesus went to eat in the house of a prominent Pharisee, he was being carefully watched. There in front of him was a man suffering from abnormal swelling of his body. Jesus asked the Pharisees and experts in the law, Is it lawful to heal on the Sabbath or not? But they remained silent. So taking hold of the man, he healed him and sent him on his way. Then he asked them, If one of you has a child or an ox that falls into a well on the Sabbath day, will you not immediately pull it out? And they had nothing to say (Luke 14:1-6).

Stretch out your hand to heal and perform signs and wonders through the name of your holy servant Jesus. After they prayed, the place where they were meeting was shaken. And they were all filled with the Holy Spirit and spoke the word of God boldly (Acts 4:30-31).

There he found a man named Aeneas, who was paralyzed and had been bedridden for eight years. Aeneas, Peter said to him, Jesus Christ heals you. Get up and roll up your mat. Immediately Aeneas got up (Acts 9:33-34).

While I am in the world, I am the light of the world. After saying this, he spit on the ground, made some mud with the saliva, and put it on the man's eyes. Go, he told him, wash in the Pool of Siloam (this word means Sent). So the man went and washed, and came home seeing. His neighbors and those who had formerly seen him begging asked, Isn't this the same man who used to sit and beg? Some claimed that he was. Others said, No, he only looks like him. But he himself insisted, I am the man. How then were your eyes opened? they asked. He replied, "The man they call Jesus made some mud and put it on my eyes. He told me to go to Siloam and wash. So I went and washed, and then I could see (John 9:5-11).

OLD TESTAMENT HEALING SCRIPTURES

He said, If you will diligently listen to the voice of the Lord your God, and do that which is right in his eyes, and give ear to his commandments and keep all his statutes, I will put none of the diseases on you that I put on the Egyptians, for I am the Lord, your healer (Exodus 15:26).

Worship the LORD your God, and His blessing will be on your food and water. I will take away sickness from among you (Exodus 23:25).

The Lord will keep you free from every disease. He will not inflict on you the horrible diseases you knew in Egypt (Deuteronomy 7:15).

See now that I, even I, am he, and there is no god beside me; I kill and I make alive; I wound and I heal; and there is none that can deliver out of my hand (Deuteronomy 32:39).

If my people who are called by my name humble themselves, and pray and seek my face and turn from their wicked ways, then I will hear from heaven and will forgive their sin and heal their land (2 Chronicles 7:14).

Have compassion on me, LORD, for I am weak. Heal me, LORD, for my bones are in agony (Psalms 6:2).

LORD my God, I called to you for help, and you healed me (Psalms 30:2).

For the LORD protects the bones of the righteous; not one of them is broken (Psalms 34:20).

The LORD will sustain him upon his sickbed; In his illness, You restore him to health (Psalms 41:3).

As for me, I said, "O Lord, be gracious to me; heal me, for I have sinned against you (Psalms 41:4).

Praise the Lord, my soul; all my inmost being, praise his holy name. Praise the Lord, my soul, and forget not all his benefits—who forgives all your sins and heals all your diseases, who redeems your life from the pit and crowns you with love and compassion, who satisfies your desires with good thing, so that your youth is renewed like the eagle's (Psalms 103:1-5).

He sent out His word and healed them, and delivered them from their destruction (Psalms 107:20).

He heals the brokenhearted and binds up their wounds (Psalms 147:3).

My son, be attentive to my words; incline your ear to my sayings. Let them not escape from your sight; keep them within your heart. For they are life to those who find them, and healing to all their flesh (Proverbs 4:20-22).

Gracious words are like a honeycomb, sweetness to the soul and health to the body (Proverbs 16:24).

A joyful heart is good medicine, but a crushed spirit dries up the bones (Proverbs 17:22).

For everything there is a season, and a time for every matter under heaven: a time to be born, and a time to die; a time to plant, and a time to pluck up what is planted; a time to kill, and a time to heal; a time to break down, and a time to build up (Ecclesiastes 3:1-3).

And the Lord will strike Egypt, striking and healing, and they will return to the Lord, and he will listen to their pleas for mercy and heal them (Isaiah 19:22).

Lord, your discipline is good, for it leads to life and health. You restore my health and allow me to live (Isaiah 38:16).

So do not fear, for I am with you; do not be dismayed, for I am your God. I will strengthen you and help you; I will uphold you with my righteous right hand (Isaiah 41:10).

But He was pierced for our transgressions, He was crushed for our iniquities; the punishment that brought us peace was on Him, and by His wounds we are healed (Isaiah 53:5).

I have seen what they do, but I will heal them anyway! I will lead them. I will comfort those who mourn, bringing words of praise to their lips. May they have abundant peace, both near and far,' says the Lord, who heals them (Isaiah 57: 18-19).

Then your light will break forth like the dawn, and your healing will quickly appear; then your righteousness will go before you, and the glory of the LORD will be your rear guard (Isaiah 58:8).

Heal me, O Lord, and I shall be healed; save me, and I shall be saved, for you are my praise (Jeremiah 17:14).

For I will restore health to you, and your wounds I will heal, declares the Lord (Jeremiah 30:17).

Behold, I will bring to it health and healing, and I will heal them and reveal to them abundance of prosperity and security (Jeremiah 33:6).

Is anyone among you sick? Let them call the elders of the church to pray over them and anoint them with oil in the name of the Lord. And the prayer offered in faith will make the sick person well; the Lord will raise them up. If they have sinned, they will be forgiven (James 5:14-15).

Dear friend, I pray that you may enjoy good health and that all may go well with you, even as your soul is getting along well (3 John 1:2).

He will wipe every tear from their eyes. There will be no more death' or mourning or crying or pain, for the old order of things has passed away (Revelations 21:4).

SCRIPTURES FOR CONSOLATION AND COMFORT

My son, pay attention to what I say; turn your ear to my words. Do not let them out of your sight, keep them within your heart; for they are life to those who find them and health to one's whole body (Proverbs 4:20-22).

A cheerful heart is good medicine, but a crushed spirit dries up the bones (Proverbs 17:22).

There is a time for everything, and a season for every activity under the heavens: a time to be born and a time to die, a time to plant and a time to uproot, a time to kill and a time to heal, a time to tear down and a time to build, a time to weep and a time to laugh, a time to mourn and a time to dance, a time to scatter stones and a time to gather them, a time to embrace and a time to refrain from embracing, a time to search and a time to give up, a time to keep and a time to throw away, a time to tear and a time to mend, a time to be silent and a time to speak, a time to love and a time to hate, a time for war and a time for peace (Ecclesiastes 3:1-8).

LORD, be gracious to us; we long for you. Be our strength every morning, our salvation in time of distress (Isaiah 33:2).

Come to me, all you who are weary and burdened, and I will give you rest. Take my yoke upon you and learn from me, for I am gentle and humble in heart, and you will find rest for your souls. For my yoke is easy and my burden is light (Matthew 11:28-30).

Peace I leave with you; my peace I give you. I do not give to you as the world gives. Do not let your hearts be troubled and do not be afraid (John 14:27).

He gives strength to the weary and increases the power of the weak (Isaiah 40:29).

No temptation has overtaken you except what is common to mankind. And God is faithful; he will not let you be tempted beyond what you can bear. But when you are tempted, he will also provide a way out so that you can endure it (1 Corinthians 10:13).

Therefore confess your sins to each other and pray for each other so that you may be healed. The prayer of a righteous person is powerful and effective (James 5:6).

He himself bore our sins in his body on the cross, so that we might die to sins and live for righteousness; by his wounds you have been healed (1 Peter 2:24).

PART TWO

Dimensional Financial Prayer

Again, the devil taketh him up into an exceeding high mountain, and sheweth him all the kingdoms of the world, and the glory of them; And saith unto him, All these things will I give thee, if thou wilt fall down and worship me (Matthew 4:8 ').

No man can serve two masters: for either he will hate the one, and love the other; or else he will hold to the one, and despise the other. Ye cannot serve God and mammon (Matthew 6:24; Luke 16:13).

If we know anything about the spirit of mammon, we must understand that the demonic Kingdom has infiltrated the monetary systems of this world to manipulate, control and rule over nations or Kingdoms and people.

This is to say that the disbursements of the monetary wealth of nations or Kingdom and people are carefully manipulated and controlled spiritually and physically to fall into some hands. There are collateral damages as nations or Kingdoms and people embrace satanic covenants to achieve glory and honor in the world stages or platforms.

The spirit of mammon is stronger and greater than any department of finance of nations or Kingdoms because this power is a ruler over nations or Kingdoms' wealth and riches as a deity. The use and sabotage of monetary or economic lifelines of nations or Kingdoms is pushing the world to the brink of disaster and total bankruptcy today. The reason is because the consolidation of the monetary systems of the world is giving the Kingdom of satan the authority and power over the monetary systems of the world. This is why many people of God have their monetary wealth locked up in the Kingdom of satan in different parts of the world until the control is broken to release their financial prosperity.

Miscalculations, wrongful estimations, faulty investments, cost of wars, and other mismanagements can take the world into the belly of the abyss or drive their economy back to the stone-age. The devaluation of the world currencies can only mean the beginning of systematically accepting other currencies until the eventual unification of all the other currencies into one basket of currency or monetary system. This is the full execution of the glory of this world -- the rulership of the Kingdom of satan over the world. In other words, the world will buy into the greatest deception of the end-times. The nations or Kingdoms of the world will accept the satanic counterfeit of the promise-land of extraordinary economic future and prosperity. And the same will apply to both a one-world government and a one-world religion.

The strategic implementation of the satanic governmental rulership will promise to offer the world governments and the people exceptional incentives of monetary success, great power, fame, influence, peace and security or eternal defense as well as honor and great abundance. The price tag will be the inauguration of the anti-Christ and the erection of idol -- false god for the world to worship, which is establishing satan's governmental rulership. Majority of the world problems stem from governmental, economical and religious unrest and the false satanic government will offer the world **the false glory** as the quick permanent solution or fix. The anti-Christ will only serve as a decoy or proxy to undermine the genuine works of God's salvation for mankind and entice the world to accept satan worship as the true worship of the Living God. (See Luke 4:5-7; Revelation 13:14-17).

People can be shut out of the the world commerce or financial systems of the world by different nations or Kingdoms and likewise, spiritual demonic powers. Nations or Kingdoms and people have ventured into the forbidden worship of false gods, time and again -- from the tower of Babel to numerous historical times. The establishment of satanic order of worship and the enforcement through imposing strict punishment against those who violate the institution -- like the days of the Babylonian, the Persian, the Greek and the Roman Empires, will deal a major blow to any attempt to oppose the rule or resist spiritually and physically.

Going back to the days of Noah will be opening the graveyards of the failed past to take away the future of humanity. Money is the artery or lifeline of the world systems of governments and targeting the three prominent areas of the human focus: government, economy and religion, is taking away the last straw to strangulate the human race. It is cutting off the life-support and withdrawing all medicinal remedies, so the people will die horrific deaths. The careful examination of these three important areas: government, economy and religion will show the depth of satan's investigative and intelligent achievements in unlocking the mysteries of the human self-governments without the LORD God.

The human escape route is hidden in Christ (the Way, the Truth and the Life) through the leadership of the Holy Spirit – the Spirit of Truth and the Spirit of Glory. However, taking away the roadmap means blinding humanity from finding their pathways to their purposes and destinies. (See 2 Corinthians 4:4). Without connecting to the Source or Author of Life, there can be no way to understand the purpose of life. Therefore, counterfeit or falsehood becomes lucrative offers to a hopeless and helpless world. A meaningless life equals to a valueless or worthless life! Because of the vulnerability of the people, they will see no reason to exercise diligence in dealing with critical issues of life and death. Satan is the spirit of death and he has thoughtfully established his Kingdom through the arts of stealing, killing and destructions. (See Genesis 3:1-6; Luke 4:5-8; John 8:44).

Nations or Kingdoms seek for alliances, however, what emboldens their forces -- authority and power are covenant agreements. It is selling the nation or Kingdom and people depending on the terms and conditions, and the duration of the agreements. The glory deals with the fullness of life so it's reaching beyond the threshold of this present age. Therefore, signing up means accepting the legal fire-sale or liquidation of the nation or Kingdom and people. Nations or Kingdoms are part of the people's inheritance because they share in the common resources and prosperity as citizens. The ground-zero of a nation or Kingdom and people starts with turning away from the LORD God and the umbrella of His covering. The withdrawal or departure of the glory is opening the whole nation or Kingdom and people to perpetual captivity and bondage.

Objects of worship are dedicated to deities that demands for special tasks or clauses for their usages. The spirit of mammon demands for worship of satan as the god and prince of this world. This is part of the integration of the systems of this world and the satanic Kingdom until everything is unified as one. (See John 12:31; 2 Corinthians 4:4). Worship requires whole sacrifice -- uncompromising obedience to orders or to serve with a person's life and resources. The word "serve" is the same as honoring the call of duty, which is to say that, money can rule a person's life. This is where the control shifts hand and instead of dictating and delegating money for good works, evil can take control to serve the interest of the god of mammon according to the Kingdom rulership of satan.

Whole sacrifice is part of the glory life; therefore, it's touching beyond the fabrics of a person's life to impact the personal investment and engagement. (See Luke 4:5-8). The disbursements and investments of the money of the world is regulated by the rulership -- the governing authority and powers, which means that satan can control the monetary systems of this world to assure that his Kingdom priorities are fully implemented.

Individual wealth and reaches as well as nations or Kingdoms' wealth and riches are greatly affected by satanic powers. Although money is part of this world, the god of this world -- spiritual dark rulers of this world have seized upon the resources of this world for their own Kingdom interests and agendas. The citizens of nations or Kingdoms can suffer great hardship when the economies are subdued and the distributions or disbursements of the wealth and riches of nations or Kingdoms are misappropriated. This is the great sacrifice that comes with the glory and its non- negotiable.

Eternal orders have no re-negotiating clauses, so often people suffer for the mistakes of their nations or Kingdoms. The rulers can enter into a deal with ruling deities or gods and sell the nation or Kingdom and the wealth and riches, thereby subjecting the people to tremendous hardship. The evils of a nation or Kingdom are distributed upon the people according to their levels and dimensions of participations, investments, engagements and commitments. Therefore, the righteous can also bear the burden in the midst of evil people. The god of money -- mammon turns the lovers of money into evil priest and kings over the people to betray their birthrights and sabotage their purposes and destinies. Evil covenants establish evil roots, so it's a revolving door of irreversible exchange that holds people under chains of bondage and captivity. The root of evil is the establishment of satanic seat of authority and power because satan is playing for keeps.

As we begin this prayer, we must understand the characteristics of Kingdoms or nations and the different cultural systems and laws that govern the people generally. Besides the individuals' cultivated behaviors, Kingdoms or nations' ways of life circulates like their monetary currencies to implicate and impact the whole society. In other words, corruption alone can impact everyone's life dramatically in a nation or Kingdom.

Kingdoms or nations exploit others -- they cheat, they steal, they violently and aggressively implement different strategies and policies to gain, even if, and when other Kingdoms or nations lose everything in the process. They defraud, they kill, and they destroy, and the consequences of such actions are re-distributed to the societies – impacting, implicating and incriminating citizens, households, businesses, organizations and the future of the people collectively.

By disconnecting yourself from the spirit of the land, and other legislative, jurisdictional and territorial authority and powers, you are breaking all ties with the systems that invite and promote deception, falsehood and corruption, and you are establishing yourself upon right-eous and moral orders. You are disassociating, disapprov-ing, rejecting, denouncing and renouncing all involvements, engagements, endorsements and support-ive participations. There are demons of patriotism – that fan the fire of hatred, racism and anarchism. You must make a spiritual and physical statement and take a stand to declare that you are not a part of the systems, and you must refuse to lend your supports, commitments and in-vestments.

Now, let us begin our prayer...

Father, in the name of Jesus Christ:

I come against every authority and power that instigate, institute, promote and use deception to corrupt and gain profitably regardless of whether it hurts my financial standing in the society or otherwise.

I come against every spiritual and physical misrepresen-tations and all illegal expenditures:

Mismanagements

False identity

Identity theft

Illegal transactions

Unauthorized financial seizures or garnishment

Asset Liquidations

Distributions

Purchases or acquisitions

Litigations, judgments, monetary awards and disbursements

Settlements of spiritual and physical legal claims and judgments

Legal fees and charges

Default fees and charges

Unaccounted and unfamiliar debts and debt payoffs

Interest charges and other fees

Maintenance or service fees and charges

Interest fees and charges

Returned instrument fees and charges

Membership fees and charges

Lawyers or advocation fees and charges

Consultation fees and charges

Bankruptcy fees and charges

I come against every false estate trustee

Financial trustee

Asset management

Banking management

Spokesperson

Authorized signer

Personal and business surrogates

I revoke every waiver signed by me consciously and unconsciously or on my behalf by anyone -- anywhere and any place, which I am unaware of -- whether spiritually, physically or otherwise in Jesus name.

Every false account that has been created and established under my identity by any agent or agency in any nation or Kingdom and destination for any purpose without my personal consent -- authorization and approval, be destroyed now in Jesus name.

Every governmental representative or assignee acting on my behalf or in my place to make any financial decision, financial budgeting, financial banking: deposits and withdrawals, asset managements, investments, acquisitions, Liquidations or disposal of properties, business, equipment, and other instruments: stocks, bonds, and any other financial market, I cut their positions off now and I force them to immediate retirement -- effective now in Jesus name.

I stop every false bill payer or manager of all operational expenses, medical expenses, insurance bills, household bills, car notes, rental bills, mortgage bills, utility bills, telecommunication bills, computers, office items, household items and all other items in Jesus name.

I serve every false trustee, surrogate, steward, spokesperson, personal and public manager, contract manager, health manager, risk manager, security manager, crisis manager, operational manager or personal and public relation manager a notice of termination now in Jesus name.

Every false voice that is speaking for me, and every voice that is representing any business or personal interest in my life and family, be silenced now in Jesus name.

Every voice that is mimicking the tone of my voice or echoing my voice -- using my voice DNA, vibration of my voice, voice recording or sound and any stored statement with my voice, cease and decease now in Jesus name.

Every decoy, impostor, familiar spirit, Kingdom agents or agencies representing me, my business and family interests falsely, anywhere and any place -- spiritually and physically, I order you removed and destroyed in Jesus name.

Any receptionist attending to my personal calls, business calls and family calls or transferring and forwarding my appointments, engagements and opportunities to different locations and contacts, I remove you now in Jesus name.

Every interpreter, translator, transcriber, and publisher communicating my life, my words and my works or that of my business and family, collapse and go out of business now in Jesus name.

Every interceptor or hijacker that is assigned to monitor and track my life, business and family's financial history, records and contractual breakthroughs, die now by fire in Jesus name.

Every falsified employment statement, employment certification or proof of employment, employment agreement or job contract as a way to usurp and gain financial benefits on my behalf, business and family, become null and void now in Jesus name.

Every document or binding waiver that extend any right to anyone -- business or individual without my personal written or verbal consent and approval, be cancelled now in Jesus name.

Every right that I or any authorized and unauthorized representative has given or delegated that invoke the action of any entity, organization, individual, nation or Kingdom to respond unilaterally or autonomously in my place or on my behalf whether spiritually or physically without further communication and consultation with me, be revoked and cut off now in Jesus name.

Every person assuming my identity: my face, my arms, my legs, my ears, my eyes, my head or any other part of me: spirit, soul and body, loose every privilege or benefit and die now in Jesus name.

Every person, agent or agency representing me or playing my role in the spirit world and any part of the world, die in my place now in Jesus name.

Every spiritual and physical body-double, impostor, familiar spirit, surrogate, advocate, guardian or ruler whether self-appointed, state appointed or actor agent, perish now in Jesus name.

Every document obtained, seized, stolen, copied, fabricated and manufactured, purchased and doctored by any agent of identity theft, I apply dimensional mark of the blood of Jesus and the power of the Holy Spirit to serve as a watermark or certificate of authenticity. I expose the bearers of such instruments to the wrath of the judgment of God in Jesus name.

I file every report: incident report, fraudulent report, illegal transaction report against you before the throne of Heaven. I authorize the arrest, prosecution and destruction of all instigators, perpetrators or criminal elements in Jesus name.

I call for spiritual and physical restitution and whole restoration now in Jesus name.

I demand for my identity to be cleared -- wiped clean and fully restored now. And every personal damage, financial damages, damages to my reputation and trustworthiness, character damages, integrity and credibility damages to be restored now in Jesus name.

Every way that spiritual deception and corruption has impacted my life, business and family! And every way that deception and corruption has tarnished my image or created distrust in my life, business and family, I recover all losses now in Jesus name.

Every unsuspected or premature withdrawal of my investment and every loss or failure in my life, business and family due to such actions, be reversed and restored now in Jesus name.

Every stagnation to my financial progress and advancement be removed now. I command my financial progress and advancement to accelerate now in Jesus name.

Every hindrance or obstacle created to hemorrhage and abort my financial maturation, be destroyed now! I call every withheld dividend, gift, favor or blessing to come forth! I receive my full harvest now in Jesus name.

Every suppression of days, nights, weeks, months and years, and every suppression of seconds, minutes and hours to create a forced delay or reverse my seasons and moments, I command everything to reset now, and I recover any and every loss in Jesus name.

Every lost opportunity, lost promotions, lost wages, lost assets, lost capitals, lost investments, lost judgments and settlements, lost deposits and credits, lost transactions and transfers, I retrieve all now -- be fully restored back to me, my business and family in Jesus name.

Every negative spiritual and physical debts created -- manipulated and controlled remotely or autonomously to reduce me, my business and family from the head to tail, from a lender to a borrower and from financial freedom to financial bondage, be destroyed now in Jesus name.

Every mysterious debt collector, debt monitor and debt service agency operating under the shadow to steal my wealth and riches and stop my financial prosperity, be completely shattered now in Jesus name.

Every legislator, executor or agents of devious laws that target my financial freedom, liberty and establishment, be destroyed now in Jesus name.

Every judge, every jury, every prosecutor, every court system and court orders that has been reached and agreed or instituted -- signed and recorded against me, my business and family, be dismissed now. I condemn every tongue that is risen again me and my finances in judgment in Jesus name. Every weapon that is formed against me and my finances I command them to malfunction and be destroyed in Jesus name.

Every financial record and history created and maintained to impact my financial life negatively or adversely and to cause unfavorable responses from the general public and private sectors, be destroyed now in Jesus name.

Every hidden mark placed on my life and my financial record or history as a tracking method -- to alert and notify any and every one in other Kingdoms or nations whether by entities, organizations or individuals, be erased now in Jesus name.

Every agent or agency employed and deployed -- assigned or commissioned to monitor my financial life for the purpose of advocating and legislating unfavorable laws to attack and cripple my financial breakthrough, go bankrupt now in Jesus name.

Every collaboration and cooperation to establish derogatory judgment against me or to profit from my financial life, be scattered now in Jesus name.

Every undertaker, buyer of debts and debt collectors that are working with any and every debt-maker to keep and maintain eternal records on me, my business and family, and to multiply adverse counsel and drive down my financial trustworthiness in the eyes of people and organizations, suffer catastrophic destruction now in Jesus name.

Every strategic agent or agency created, planted and assigned to purposefully undermine my financial rise or to cause my finances to fail, receive your judgment -- fall now and never rise again in Jesus name.

Every secret buyer of my debts, be revealed and settled now in Jesus name.

Every entity, organization, individual, Kingdom or nation that is banking on profiting from my financial loss or failures, fail and totally bankrupt now in Jesus name.

Every corporation, organization, entity, person and every place that the enemy has used my identity or acted as my authorized representative, authorized signer, a surrogate or employed agent and agency to establish any personal and business relationships, accounts, transactions or other engagements to implicate, complicate and incriminate my life, business and family, suffer mysterious destruction now in Jesus name"

Every spiritual and physical investigator, conspirator, motivator, accomplice or cheerleader that incite, recruit and drive people or organizations to hurt my financial life, be annihilated in Jesus name.

Every watchman, witches and warlocks or Wiccan that carry out satanic Kingdom orders or assignments to fight against my financial rising, fall down and die now in Jesus name.

Every financial death squad, assassinator, terminator, thieves, killers and destroyers, meet your destruction now in Jesus name.

Every false and strange next of kin, heirs, custodians, stewards, trustees, enforcers of written or oral statement of will, be removed now in Jesus name.

Every governmental rulership authority and power giving orders to seize, possess, take into custody or control of my wealth and riches, be destroyed now in Jesus name.

Every law or decree from any rulership authority and power that is creating financial embargoes and sanctions against my life, business and family because of my opposition or resistance to the rulership orders, judgments and decrees, be lifted now.

I overcome any and every retaliation and enforcement in Jesus name.

Every reporter, every spy, every informant and every witness that is cooperating and collaborating with any agency or institution, governmental authority and power to bring accusations against me, my business and family, suffer mighty destruction now in Jesus name.

Every financial sabotage, misplacement, misappropriation and reversal of fortune to create significant loss of wealth and riches, and subject my life, business and family to extreme financial hardship, be wasted now. I command everything to be recovered and credited back now in Jesus name.

Every monetary institution withholding my personal money, business money and family money, and every warehouse storing up my wealth and riches, I order you closed now. I release and I receive all my money now in Jesus name.

Every trademark, service mark and copyright of my name established under my business or family name and business by all agents or agencies, surrogates, representatives, authorized signers, financial institutions or otherwise, I litigate against all infringements and damages now in Jesus name.

I revoke and I reclaim all documents bearing such trademarks, service marks and copyrights now in Jesus name.

I recover all disbursements and reimbursements to any person or persons, organizations and entities, spiritually and physically in Jesus name.

Every security system or apparatus that is installed, armed and engaged, and every security agent and agency employed and deployed to monitor or watch over my wealth and riches, be dismantled and decimated now in Jesus name.

I command every wealth transfer to break forth and materialize in my life, business and family now in Jesus name.

Every environmental disaster and atmospheric catastrophe targeting my life, business life and family life, stop now in Jesus name.

Every entity, organization, corporation, Kingdom or nation and people that have withdrawn or withheld their business relationships and supports from me, my business, and family, be reinstated and normalized now in Jesus name.

Anywhere and any place that I have been personally blacklisted, or my business name and family name has been discredited and mislabeled, be completely restored now in Jesus name.

I close every false bank account now

I close every false personal account now

I close every false business account now

I close every false family account now

I liquidate every existing asset now

I cease and withdraw every available resource in those accounts now in Jesus name

I terminate every false CFO over my life, business and family now

I terminate every false CEO over my life, business and family now

I terminate every false manager over the affairs of my life, business and family now

I terminate every false authorized signer over my financial life, business financial life and family financial life now

I terminate every false planner over my life, business and family now

I terminate every false advisor, counselor, and risk management officer over my life, business and family now

I terminate every false personal banker, business banker, family banker, investor, broker and acquisition director or officer now

You are all fired, effective immediately, wherever you are based or operating from in Jesus name.

I declare that I am exempt from any spiritual and physical liability -- restitution and punitive damages created as a result of false representatives, surrogates, unauthorized personal, business and family signers.

I declare that I am not responsible, liable or accountable for any criminal financial damages to anyone, organization, person, Kingdom or nation as a result of any misrepresentation, misinformation, fraudulent acts, deception and corruption or other financial mischiefs -- spiritually and physically.

I declare openly that any use of my identity falsely whether in part or in full to obtain any financial service or benefit in any Kingdom or nation and from anyone without my personal consent and approval is a spiritual and physical criminal act. Therefore, I authorize the arrest, prosecution and condemnation of any and all participants or perpetrators in Jesus name.

I declare openly that any use of my image or form -- anything bearing my resemblance or similitude as a representation of me, my business and family is a spiritual and physical criminal act and therefore, subject to criminal prosecution, imprisonment, restitution and restoration in Jesus name.

I declare a new beginning -- a fresh start in my financial life, my business life, and my family life now in Jesus name.

I declare that I am now a financial magnet -- a financial attraction to the world: businesses, organizations, entities, communities, individuals, Kingdoms or nations across the world in Jesus name.

I declare that I am now in great demand and highly sought after, everywhere -- spiritually, physically and otherwise in Jesus name.

I declare that I am a living miracle, signs and wonder to my generation and the world: every Kingdom, every nation and all people in Jesus name.

I declare that my financial life is fully restored and established permanently from now forward in Jesus mighty name.

PART THREE

Dynamic Warfare Prayer

FATHER, IN THE NAME OF JESUS:

I confess that Jesus Christ is My LORD and Savior.

I confess that Jesus Christ gave His life and shed His blood for me on the Cross of Calvary.

I confess that the blood of Jesus Christ has washed all my sins, and that I am now made righteous through Him.

I confess that my sins have been forgiven, and I am born again – saved, sealed with the Holy Spirit of Adoption, filled with the Holy Spirit of promise, and clothed upon with power.

I confess that I have received power to walk in the newness of life in Christ. I am now free as a child of God in Jesus name.

I confess that I have been translated from the kingdom of darkness into the kingdom of light – the Kingdom of the dear Son of God in Jesus name.

I denounce and renounce every satanic and occultism -- demonic covenants, initiations, links, associations and attachments.

I denounce and renounce every ancestral demonic spirit from my grandfather, grandmother, father, mother or any other source including every curse stemming from their lineages and roots.

I denounce and renounce every witch and warlock encounter and consultation or business transactions and exchanges.

I denounce and renounce every witchcraft participation and practices or rituals.

I denounce and renounce every astrological contact, zodiac, tarot reading, palm reading, psychic reading, fortune-telling, divination, false prophetic exposures in any shape or form – spiritually, physically and otherwise.

I denounce and renounce necromancy – consultation and communication with the spirit of the death, astral projection, telepathy, extra-sensory perception, clairvoyance, and transcendental meditation.

I denounce and renounce every demonic vision, dreams, trances and every form of demonic mediums, contacts and exchanges of information, gifts, relationships, and businesses.

I denounce and renounce satanic and demonic familiarity, acquaintance and attraction to my life, family, ministry, business – anything that connects us to exchange any form of spiritual or physical views, whether political, religious or other engagements.

I denounce and renounce every satanic – demonic marriage relationship, business agreement, alliance or other forms of contractual obligations and contacts.

I denounce and renounce every satanic enchantment, rituals, ceremonies, sacrifices, worship, whether spiritual or physical.

I denounce and renounce every consent, acceptance and approval of any document that relates or pertains to demonic partnership, friendship, investment, business or social arrangements.

I denounce and renounce every oath of service, inauguration, commemoration and allegiance to satan and the kingdom of darkness.

I denounce and renounce every commitment and dedication to serve satan and his demons, whether subjective, voluntary or obligation and mandate of the law of the kingdom of darkness.

I denounce and renounce any office, position, wages or benefits, favors and promotion in rank that are satanically designed or orchestrated by demons to entrap and bound me in captivity.

I denounce and renounce all doors of opportunity that demonic powers have opened as a way to detour, distract and confuse my life or the will and purpose of God.

I denounce and renounce every consultation or contacts with demonic representatives–agents and agencies or institutions that transact the business of, or serve the interest of the governmental ruler-ship of the kingdom of satan.

I denounce and renounce every spiritual demonic husband, wife, children, friends, associates, loved ones that satan is using to reach or contact me spiritually and physically.

I denounce and renounce any satanic chieftaincy or other titles linked to my name.

I denounce and renounce every satanic slavery, colonization and destabilization to possess, oppress, manipulate and control my life and destiny.

I denounce and renounce every spiritual intimacy: sexual contacts with demons or human agents through the computer, television, magazines, newspapers, or other means, whether oral sex, anal sex, vaginal penetration, masturbation, homosexual act, lesbianism, bestiality, or any form of sodomy.

I denounce and renounce all subjective practices to honor satan and demons or human agents and agencies as a way to gain prosperity – accumulate wealth and riches, or achieve fame and publicity.

I denounce and renounce every herbalist ritual – witches and warlocks prescribed remedy: charms or amulets to save, cure, deliver, protect, defend, provide, secure and materialize any type of blessing or to curse by casting spells to harm others.

I denounce and renounce every satanic projection of wickedness, evil and atrocities against my life as a conduit to affect and infect others in Jesus name.

I dedicate and commit my life – spirit, soul and body to the Father, Son and the Holy Spirit.

I dedicate and commit my husband, or wife, children and household to the Father, Son and the Holy Spirit.

I dedicate and commit my talents, gifts, dreams and visions.

I dedicate and commit my finances, job, ministry, business, career and goals.

I dedicate and commit my going out and coming in, my days and my nights, my waking up and my going to bed.

I dedicate and commit my thought life, imagination, emotions, will and body in Jesus name.

I dedicate and commit my past, present and future – my destiny and all I am or will ever become in this life and the life to come for His glory in Jesus name.

I oppose before Heaven and earth every legislative decree, laws or judgments that approve and validate evil for righteousness.

I oppose and reject the perversion of the rightful ways of the LORD.

I declare that I have chosen the ways of the LORD God for my life and my household – for me and my house, we will worship the LORD and only Him will we serve forever.

I declare by the decree of the LORD God for such legislative body and orders to be brought to nothing. And I call for such legislative authority and powers to fall in Jesus name.

I legislate against evil counsel, ungodly rulership, spiritual and physical enforcement agents and agencies, and I declare in the name of Jesus that they must fall.

I subpoena for the end of their reign and for their positions to be taken away by another in Jesus name.

I speak to the foundations and pillars of their authority and powers to bow down and subject to the name of Jesus Christ.

I speak to the ground under their structures to give way, and I decree the reign of righteousness to overtake their establishment.

I call for their days to fail and their nights to disappear.

I call for their seasons and times to be removed and their plans to be confused in the name of Jesus.

I oppose the band of the wicked and evil-doers, and I raise up the banner of holiness and righteousness over nations and kingdoms.

I call for the reign of the Kingdom of God and the supreme ruler-ship of the Kingdom of Heaven.

I declare the invasion of Heaven over the earth and the revelation of the throne of the LORD God to rule with all authority and power.

I come against imperial powers – the spirit of Pharaoh and the rulership orders of his decrees or judgment against my life and the purpose of Heaven.

I come against all the enforcement and execution of the task masters and evil slave masters that are delegated with Pharaoh's authority and power to torment my life with hard labors. The Bible said, the blessing of the LORD makes rich and there is no added sorrow.

I oppose and reject every conscious and sub-conscious allegiance to the spirit of Pharaoh and the government of Pharaoh, and I declare that I am not subject under the spirit of the land.

I come against every demonic giants and goliath agents that terrorize, intimidate and frighten to undermine and humiliate.

I come against the spirit of Jezebel – the retaliatory armies and avengers assigned against the prophets of God and the prophetic voices and orders over the land.

I come against all deception and lies – spiritual identity theft that is intended to sabotage my integrity and credibility by incriminating and polluting my glory in Christ Jesus.

I declare that my spiritual and physical identity is secured under the covenant of the blood of Jesus Christ and Heaven's diplomatic immunity.

I call for Heaven's vigorous response wherever my name is mentioned or called up.

I call for the Kingdom authority and power of Heaven to fully investigate and recover all my images, personal belongings and family properties – all my blessings that the enemy and the agents have intercepted and stolen or being used anywhere without my verbal, written authorization or contractual agreement and the consent or approval of the Father, Son and the Holy Spirit in Jesus Name.

I oppose every contrary order to the ruler-ship decrees and judgments of God over the earth.

I call for the release of the authority and power of Heaven to establish eternal order over the creation in Jesus name.

I speak to the elements of God's creation to align themselves in unified rebellion to oppose all evil orders of the kingdom of darkness and the kingdoms of the world.

I oppose every constitution and legislation that undermine, neglect and reduce the righteous value of the judgment of the LORD GOD over the earth – the nations or kingdoms and people.

I call for every evil order to steal, to kill and to destroy to be settled by the fire of the judgment of God.

I bring nations or kingdoms and people under the subjection of the authority and power of God Almighty and All-powerful.

I call for the light of God to reveal all darkness, and to free those that are chained in bondage through ignorance.

I call for evil roots to be dismantled and wicked works to the destroyed in Jesus name.

I call every wandering focus to be restored, and every damaged hope and shattered life, dreams and visions to be restored in Jesus name.

I declare the salvation of the LORD over homes, businesses, territories, cites, states, nations or kingdoms.

I call for supernatural shifting's that will alter the balance of spiritual and physical authority and powers and change the direction or trajectory of people's lives everywhere.

I decree judgment over every stubborn element that stand against spiritual shifting and true godly hunger and thirst – real spiritual change and transformation.

I terminate every order of evil assignments, and I declare the victory of the LORD today in Jesus name.

I raise up the flag of the blood of Jesus Christ over enemy territories and jurisdictions or domains of rulership, and I call forth the great harvest of the LORD.

I call up the armies of God's reservists – the creation to rise up for the moment and seal every victory and conquer.

Let them match in dominion against every force of darkness and agents or agencies that uphold the constitution of the ruler-ship of the kingdom of satan.

Let there be no places for them to run or hide from the anger and wrath of God Almighty and All-powerful.

Let the creation witness and testify against their hiding places or positions, and let their immunities be taken away from them.

Let there be a shaking and quaking, and mighty thundering and lightning, and let the voice of God come with great authority and power to discomfort and disgrace the camps of the enemy in Jesus name.

I command the rotation of the earth to move according to the alignment and order of Heaven.

I command every life, household, business and destiny that has been confused, destabilized, sabotaged or turned upside-down to be reversed now, and begin to move in the right spiritual and physical direction according to the purpose of God in Jesus name.

I command every purpose that has been affected by demonic authority and powers, agents, agencies or pressures of life to be prioritized according to the mandate of Heaven.

I command spiritual and physical infections that stigmatize and corrupt to create abnormalities: negative side-effects, sicknesses, diseases, ailments, illnesses to dry up from the roots and be healed in Jesus name.

I command all circumstances created or manipulated and controlled by spiritual and physical armed forces – agents and agencies of darkness to be liberated in Jesus name.

I command every life that is tormented, depressed, suppressed, afflicted and bereaved to be released now in Jesus name.

I command every dream, vision and hope that has been tarnished to be restored. I command every curse to be broken, and I call favors to overtake the lives of the people of God everywhere.

I command prosperity to heal the wounds, hurts and pains of disadvantages, misfortunes, poverty and lack in Jesus name.

I command the power of resurrection to destroy the power of death over the lives and situations of the people of God now.

I command the power of creation to create – make everything new and the power of revelation to reveal everything that is hidden in the spirit realm of life.

Let there be a breaking forth, materialization and actualization of those things that Heaven has released in Jesus name.

I command darkness to move away and light to break forth, and I call for new beginnings over the lives of the people of God.

I command the elements of God's creation to reject every alliance, offers, appeals, rewards, and to resist every pressure to compromise or submit to evil authority and powers to fight against my life and destiny in Jesus name.

Let the forces of the enemy be stranded and disappointed without any support or assistance from anywhere in the spiritual and physical universes.

Let their plans be disturbed and disrupted, and let them suffer great deterioration and bankruptcy in Jesus name.

I command the release of the fullness of the authority and power of God to overtake the earth and release people by the thousands and millions in Jesus name.

I command the earth to receive the revelation of God and the regulatory orders of His decrees and judgments.

Let the power of evil hide from the face of the earth and let the forces of evil run away, and let the harvest of the people of God be released in Jesus name.

I command the heat of the sun and the fire of hell not to touch the people of God, and I command their lives to shine forth by the light of God.

I command their shame to be turn into glory, and I call forth success and prosperity to bless their works in Jesus name.

I exercise my Heaven given authority and power to bind, and I restrain all enemy strike forces: opposing authority and powers, attack groups, retaliatory expedition teams – every demonic chain and ranks, satanic informants, spies and other agents or agencies representing the interest of the kingdom ruler-ship of satan.

I restrain their mobility, and I block every pathway to their missions or assignments.

I cut off the airspaces, the waterways, the land-spaces, the human points of contact and other secret avenues.

I stop every agent or agency that is assigned to collaborate and corroborate with demonic powers in fulfilling the kingdom mandate of satan.

I block all designs, methods, systems and other intelligent measures used to gather and collect intelligence against my life, family, business and ministry.

I speak to the enemy's instruments of war to expire through malfunction and dysfunction. The Bible said that no weapons formed against me shall prosper.

I silence every tongue that is risen up against me in judgment.

I condemn it in the name of Jesus, and I declare it unauthorized and unqualified to speak over my life and the affairs that relate to my destiny.

I command every open case against me, my family and business to be dismissed, dissolved and sealed by the blood of Jesus Christ in Jesus name.

I speak to every door of vulnerability and victimization, sabotage, betrayal or opportunity that will serve to the enemy's advantage over my life and destiny to be closed and sealed in Jesus name.

I lose and release my guardian angels, warrior angels and other host of God's armies to intervene according to the plan of the Will and purpose of the LORD God for my life.

I call for the release of Heaven's super weapons of war to demolish any fortification and uproot the strongholds of the enemy in Jesus name.

I cut off every enemy's escape route, and I restrain all free movements of enemy troops, intelligence apparatus, communication devises, combat gears and armories – spiritually and physically in Jesus name.

I restrain the seasons and time zones to confuse the enemy's plans of arrangements and order of engagements.

I release extreme spiritual and physical adverse weather and temperature conditions to undermine every enemy's operation.

I speak to the elements of God's creation to become extremely hostile and aggressively resistant to the enemy forces – spiritually and physically in Jesus name.

I speak to the elements of God's creation to release their defenses to stop the expedited and accelerated responses of the enemy's forces.

Let there be spiritual tsunami, earthquakes, thunderstorms, lightning, flood, hail, snowstorm, windstorm, volcanic eruption and fire.

Let the wonders of the LORD God increase and multiply to surpass all weapons of the enemy to destroy their powers and effects.

Let the elements of God's creation go on the highest spiritual and physical alert to monitor and destroy the armies of darkness in Jesus name.

Let there be total blockades in every passage way that connect the spirit realm to the natural or the physical to the spirit realm.
Let there be spiritual blackouts in the kingdoms of the enemy to disorient the advancing plans of the forces of evil in Jesus name.

Let nature fight with overwhelming intensity and aggressiveness to defend against the throne of the rulership of Heaven and the purpose of the LORD God Almighty and All-powerful over my life.

Let the creation of the LORD God declare His glory in Jesus mighty name.

HOW TO USE WEAPONS OF DIMENSIONAL WARFARE

*The LORD is a **man of war**: the LORD is his name* (Exodus 15:3).

Transformation is the norms of the glory life: man came out of the dust of the earth. The material creation came out of the immaterial. The physical came out of the spiritual. The transitions between these dimensions are ever changing and transforming all things. In epic spiritual battles throughout the Bible, we have numerous accounts of unconventional weapons that defy all logics and expectations. The people of God must look beyond the natural limitations and explore the spiritual dimensions where the origin of life came. The creative power of God is a secret phenomenon and yet, some people are finding the keys, like Moses and others who experienced the deeper depths of God. The Bible said, for with God nothing shall be impossible. The impacts of some spiritual weapons of warfare could be extremely devastating. I must say that we are at the edge of unusual shift to bring our generation into the age of the supernatural. Many people will unlock the hidden mysteries of the end-times and find great power to do great exploits. Epic warfare will be fought again and again before the end of all things. The role players are going to cross the threshold of this life to blend into the next dimensions of life. Keys to the uncommon are always protected and handed only to those who will exercise diligent caution to maintain the highest level of integrity and credibility. This is why everything is tried and tested before the commissioning and establishment!

Every nation or kingdom is dressed for war whether they are only rehearsing or preparing their weapons. The rehearsal is not a choir practice but a war in the making. Weapons of war are created for purpose and a kingdom is purpose-driven so weaponizing the created works is beyond logical. A man of war is a man who is intrigued by concepts of warfare and fascinated by creating instrument of war. Heaven incubates treasures of extraordinary weapons of warfare -- such as no nation or kingdom has ever seen. The difference is that infinite and eternal weapons are not designed for periodic upgrades and updates. They are not designed to malfunction or age according to the numbers of years! The reason is that any lapse can cause irreparable breaches! There are no rooms for diagnostic approaches to resolving issues in infinity and eternity so everything must be transparent. The light nature takes away the extra weights of material components and solve the issues of gravity. The lives of spiritual beings and elements are light in nature besides being illuminated to add exceptional transparency like holographic and super-imposed images. This is the nature of incorporeal—the crossroad of material and immaterial. The sudden realization: The exposure of secret or hidden things whether by appearing and disappearing is what the power of revelation brings in dimensional spiritual warfare. Objects, subjects and elements momentarily gravitate—ascend and descend. Things are created that never existed and whatever is dead rise or resurrect to life. The acceleration of all things combined with the agility and flexibility of all created works, makes the spirit realms far superior to external or physical life. Dynamic power of prayer is masterful articulations of secret weapons of glory in dimensional warfare. To help you embrace the shift and quickly adjust to the twilights of the infinite and eternal revelation of the LORD God and the mysteries of His great power, many weapons of unusual categories have been carefully listed below. We have done the legworks to give you some important overviews and practical engagement of these ultimate or apocalyptic weapons. Therefore, let us examine the libraries and explore the catalogues of heaven's dimensional weapons.

FIERY SERPENTS AND MORE -- *And the LORD sent fiery serpents among the people, and they bit the people; and much people of Israel died* (Numbers 21:6).

Who led thee through that great and terrible wilderness, wherein were fiery serpents, and scorpions, and drought, where there was no water; who brought thee forth water out of the rock of flint (Deuteronomy 8:15).

Fiery serpents are equipped with firepower weapons that burn uncontrollably and cannot be cured with external remediation. This is why spiritual attacks kill and destroy peoples' lives every day. The time it would take to research and invent a medicinal cure becomes too late for the victim to continue to live. The poison of this biblical serpent has added element to cause death blow without cure. Therefore, if the event is to be repeated today, the same effect will be realized. People will die because of the bites without medicinal cure. The same applies to scorpions and spiritual draught. The things that would normally happen with scorpion sting in the natural happen in the spirit and the pain has no physical cure. Similarly, spiritual draught releases unbearable anguish into the soul -- affecting a person's life with internal and external agony. Draught on the other hand, is withdrawing anything that supports the comfort of life. Mineral resources are life ingredients -- and withholding or withdrawing them is like taking away medicine from a patient that is near death. Life support can be turned off to induce physical death and likewise, some spiritual impacts can devastate a whole person. Spiritual poisons exist and they are applied from spiritual perspectives with physical consequences. This is part of why the knowledge of evil was hidden from the first perfect man in the glory because the glory is the perfection of all knowledge. Perfection here means the application and implementation according to the counsel and judgment of the LORD God, which does not incur additional penalties.

SHIELD, SPEAR AND JAVELIN - *And the LORD said unto Joshua, Stretch out the spear that is in thy hand toward Ai; for I will give it into thine hand. And Joshua stretched out the spear that he had in his hand toward the city* (Joshua 8:18).

SPEAR - *Draw out also the spear, and stop the way against them that persecute me: say unto my soul, I am thy salvation* (Psalms 35:3).

JAVELIN - *And Saul cast the javelin; for he said, I will smite David even to the wall with it. And David avoided out of his presence twice* (1 Samuel 18:11).

Please do not let the orthodox nature of these ancient weapons fool you to believe that they are outdated because we are in a technological age. This generation is not more advanced than the ancient times. The power of any civilization is determined by the depth of spirituality. The greatness is measured by the historical endurance or they will quickly fade away. The greater civilization will see the greater spiritual influence! It is why rising and falling is a race against time. As far apart as civilizations have come, each has left a history and a legacy even if it was only a charred bone! The endurance of these weapons from the archives of the Bible indicates that their times of use are not yet over. Besides fighting spiritual warfare, I am an admirer of weapons of warfare so I spend time examining the makeup and the power of ultimate weapons, especially as we come to the edge of the end-times. Spiritual weapons of warfare are not retired in the museums -- they are not collectable items because they are never outdated. They are as effective today as eternity can remember. You must revisit the days of the old to glean from the archives of historical brave warriors, who looked at the face of death and stood their grounds. With their eyes deeming with fear of death, they overthrow the sting of death. It is noteworthy, to take a closer look at the weapons they used that pieced the hearts of the enemies. Those weapons included shields, spears and javelins -- anointed or enhanced by the Spirit. Mighty weapons arc born in the Spirit because they are created by the Almighty and All-powerful. I want you to remember this: weapons that are not man-made are not controlled by men even when they are placed in the hands of men or handled by men! For the weapons of our warfare are not carnal but mighty through God to the pulling down of strongholds. (See 2 Corinthians 10:1-5). **The armors of the LORD may look foolish but they are the last weapons that remain standing after having done all! Ask the LORD to release these weapons against the enemy in the heart of close combat and let their blood run like water. Spare no soldier and never turn away from your breakthrough!** *Thou shalt burn with fire a third part in the midst of the city, when the days of the siege are fulfilled: and thou shalt take a third part, and smite about it with a knife: and a third part thou shalt scatter in the wind; and I will draw out a sword after them* (Ezekiel 5:3).

STARS -- *They fought from heaven; the stars in their courses fought against Sisera* (Judges 5:8, 20).

The stars are orbital weapons like the sun and the moon. They use their rays or light to see like target acquisition systems. They operate similar to radars, sensors, cameras, satellites and GPS tracking to lock-in on their targets. The people of God have allowed the enemy to feel comfortable around God's catastrophic weapons of warfare. Dimensional warfare is not only spiritual but physical besides having dual usages. They can serve the human interest and burn the enemy and it is absolutely normal with military products. The humans live normal lives and serve in the military to kill and destroy. The weapons likewise protect and kill and destroy. The enemy targets the stars of people for good reasons, which is to first identify whose star and establish the identity of the individual person. A strategy is devised to approach with caution to present the person with an offer or terminate him or her upon contact. The sun, moon and star are guidance because they illuminate to reveal so they can be consulted or utilized for direction. Nevertheless, we must not forget that they are weaponized to fight for the purpose of God, not only for their lives but anywhere the purpose of God is revealed. They can be commanded by the authority and power of the LORD God to turn on the enemy. If the enemy try to capture your star, you must turn your star into a star war! The constellation is a gallery that showcase hidden mysteries of the luminaries. Both the demonic kingdom and the world share common interest in observing what is happening up there. Often, they share intelligence and collaborate. They target their enemies using their guidance or assets based on those locations. Like the spiritual warfare like the physical warfare. There are demonic powers above the earth atmosphere and there are world military assets that are constantly orbiting the earth atmosphere. They are all parts of the guiding systems that target nations or kingdoms and people. Your job is to activate the epic weapons of the created works of God and turn them against the powers of the enemy -- the nations or kingdoms and people that embrace the kingdom of satan and cooperate to destroy your life and other people's lives. The earth is the LORD's and the fullness thereof. The sun can strike them by day and the moon by night and the stars can fight them. **Pray and command the sun and the moon and the stars to become laser weapons by increasing their lights and heatwaves against the enemy. Blind the eyes of the enemies and take away their sights or visions. Deprive them the abilities to function in the day and operate in the night. Bring blizzards upon them and cause different storms to chase them with life threatening dangers everywhere. Cripple their devices and electrocute their monitoring devices. Destroy their apparatus spiritually and physically and destabilize their mobilities. Create extreme weather conditions on their pathways and cut off their advancement and assignments. Target their command posts and territories or domains.** This is what Adam did not do, which you must now do for the glory of the LORD God through Jesus Christ.

WEATHER - *Fair weather cometh out of the north: with God is terrible majesty* (Job 37:22).

The majestic glory of God is the dimension where the LORD God exposes the secret weapons embedded within the chambers of elements as well as the abilities of the elements to engage in warfare for his purpose. Like automation or command and control, the LORD God can activate elements for war including using the elements or arming them for battles. Giving orders to the created

works and equipping them to behave in the nature prescribed according to God's will and purpose is beyond
carrying around armored tanks and aircraft carriers. The
majestic glory is part of curtailing the great powers of elements until they are authorized by the LORD of Hosts
and Captain of the Host. Inventory of weapons are seat-
ing ducks in the case of war even if they have mobility or
defensive mechanisms or added weaponry. The more
pieces of components are assembled together are the
more vulnerable they become. Hidden weapons are more
deadly and the sudden introduction is a heartbreaker.
The enemy would not know what to expect and how to
prepare for the unexpected. This is why revelation is
greater than inspiration and discernment! The weapon-
ization of elements in the glory is epic strategy to deal
with epic battles. The impossible is inexhaustible because
everything keeps unfolding and realtime events present
indefensible scenarios that even the most formidable
army cannot challenge or change the balance of power.
"Arise and shine" shows how sudden things unfold in the
glory and the revelation shifts the calculation of all ar-
ranged preparations. Balance of power is changed by introduction of hidden weapons of epic power so the
enemy is forced to withdraw or perish. Jesus said, *I saw
satan like lightning fall from heaven* (Luke 10:18). You can
also look at Revelation 12:7-9. **You must pray for the
LORD God to change the balance of power to favor
your advancement against the enemy and scatter them.
You can terrorize the enemy with the trembling fear of
the LORD God by calling down the glory of God into
your battles!** See more of the revelation of the majestic
glory here: (Psalms 18:6-14).

FOOT AND BEAST - *And forgetteth that the foot may
crush them, or that the wild beast may break them* (Job
39:15).

I love the intensity and extremity of these merciless weapons of warfare. When the people heard the noise of terrible armies matching toward their City, not knowing that it was only four lepers, they abandoned the City. (See 2 Kings 7:5-8). They fled without spending time to remove the spoils and the spoils fell into the hands of the people of God. In many places of religious worships around the world, you will see why there are often stampedes and many people sacrifice their lives. Stampede is using multiple foot soldiers and beasts to match people down -- trample them with several repeated blows until they die. I have seen in the spirit where spiritual animals are released upon Cities and people had to run for their lives because these evil animals kill and destroy their victims as they roam around. The enemy deploys these evil animals to attack people causing them death and destruction. We also see where people were attacked by animals in the Bible as well as physically today around the world. As in the spirit so also in the natural world. Driving elements, animals and objects with great force and colliding with people is part of brutal force to harm them. Some places of special interests in the spirit realms whether in the realms of God or the demonic kingdom are protected and defended by different creatures including animals. Some of these animals are prehistoric, which is to say that the enemy is using their images and identities because they are physically extinct. The same way the movie industries can recreate the images of these lost beasts, the demonic kingdom is full of illusion and deception. In the glory realms, you subdue and rule by increase and multiplication or numerically and strength. You can command the animals whether in the land, the air and the water -- spiritually and physically because Adam had dominion. (See Genesis 1:26-28). The animals' kingdom was not inhabited by mere pets but armies of unusual power. **Call for stampede upon your enemy and**

trample their Cities, territories and domains. Destroy their infrastructure and collapse their civilization. This is the authority and power of the sons of God like Adam and the Second Adam -- the Son of God! This is what happened in Sodom and Gomorrah and the world of Noah besides other places the judgment of God came. The Bible said, *the boar out of the wood doth waste it, and the wild beast of the field doth devour it* (Psalms 80:13).

MIGHTY POWER - *He teacheth my hands to war; so that a bow of steel is broken by mine arms* (2 Samuel 22:35).

Who is this King of glory? The LORD strong and mighty, the LORD mighty in battle (Psalms 24:8).

The Bible said, be strong in the LORD and the power of his might (Ephesians 6:10). Again, it's not by power nor by might and the Spirit of the LORG God is the Spirit of Might (Zechariah 4:6). The Spirit of God as the Spirit of Might and the Spirit of Glory shows a dynamic shift between degree of strength and the fullness of the mighty power of God -- the power of the Highest! (See Luke 1:35). Mighty weapons are overloaded with mighty power to make the weapon unstoppable and indefensible. You cannot wrestle it down, hold it down, tie it up, stand on the pathway, erect security barriers or defenses around it. You are practically dealing with something that cannot be tamed. This is why it is not by might nor by power. The Bible said, for with God, nothing shall be impossible (Luke 1:37). Some battles in the spirit realms are not fought by humans -- no matter how high or deep they may be. They will need angelic intervention, they will need the LORD God and the revelation of his majestic glory or simply, commanding elements to unleash their epic weapons of war. Anything or a person whether angels, humans, animals and elements that the mighty power of God comes upon or invades becomes weapons of epic catastrophe. Unless the LORD God calls them back, nothing will be able to stop them and nothing will be left standing on their paths of destruction! Mighty power is raw strength without restrain so it is dealing beyond who is standing in front of you or what you are seeing. The mighty power of God is so incredible and terrible that it is a weapon of annihilation. It terrifies the enemy and terrorizes the camp or kingdom of the enemy regardless of how organized, how powerful, how many they are numerically and whatever weapons they may possess. They have no bearing whatsoever and they are not counted as any impediment or obstacle to the purpose of the LORD! Pray for the mighty power of God to make you stronger than any enemy -- spiritually and physically like David, Samson and the rest, etc. The mighty power of the LORD God is the greatest weapon of warfare because it is what makes every other weapon of spiritual warfare stronger than the enemies' weapons. When the Spirit of God overtakes any weapon of warfare whether spiritual or physical, the weapon becomes matchless to any other weapon. The reason is that the power of God is immeasurable and therefore, Almighty and All-powerful!

REPROOF - *When they were but a few men in number, Yea, very few, and sojourners in it. And they went about from nation to nation, From one kingdom to another people. He suffered no man to do them wrong; Yea, he reproved kings for their sakes* (Psalms 105:12 14).

A reproof is an expression of blame or disapproval. This word can be paired together with the words: rebuke, reprimand, reproach and admonishment. A warning to stop someone from taking certain action to avoid the consequential aftermath or incurring a bitter repercussion. The side-effect of the blowback can become excessively damaging. Therefore, we must refrain from taking such action. God can speak to people including the enemy on your behalf to warn them and stop them from harassing and antagonizing you. This is part of his favors. His favor is bestowed upon his people so it's not abnormal to see his reaction and interaction with your enemy. Your warning to the enemy can be conveyed through order means but the LORD can intervene on the matter personally. Angels can be sent on your behalf. Your prayers for God's intervention carry great weight and the fervency of your prayers compound the strength of your power with God. This is why some enemies don't want to mess around with some people of God while some people of God are constantly under the enemy's harassment and aggression. You must fight your enemy or at least report his illegal abusive behaviors to the LORD to bring consequences upon them. Your enemies must not feel vindicated and free to act with impunity to antagonize and sabotage your life. You must draw the line on the sand and define what rules your enemies must follow or they will not know where to stop. If they feel they have advantage over you, they will not listen to your warnings nor hearken to your cries. Therefore, when the LORD confronts your enemy, it is beyond speaking in a thousand tongues or fasting and praying forever. It is the ultimate answer to all your labors because you will not have to warn your enemies over and over again or repeatedly! It is putting the nail on the coffin to bury the voices of your enemies! The voice of the LORD God is not what the enemy forgets so quickly because those words will not return void so the consequences are too great to just ignore. The voice of God's rebuke traumatizes the enemy with the great fear of the LORD, and it is why the enemy shrink and cease from unnecessary adventures against the people of God or they will continue to pressure them. **You must pray until you hear the voice of the LORD God and until you provoke Him to respond to your enemy with his voice to settle your case. Your enemy must know that God is for you or they will mistake his silence as abandonment and rejection.** This is why they mock the people of God that their God has forsaken them! The Bible said, *What then shall we say to these things? If God is for you,* *who is against us* (Romans 8:31).

HISS - *And he will lift up an ensign to the nations from far, and will hiss unto them from the end of the earth: and, behold, they shall come with speed swiftly* (Isaiah 5:26).

And it shall come to pass in that day, that the LORD shall hiss for the fly that is in the uttermost part of the rivers of Egypt, and for the bee that is in the land of Assyria. In the same day shall the Lord shave with a razor that is hired, namely, by them beyond the river, by the king of Assyria, the head, and the hair of the feet: and it shall also consume the beard (Isaiah 7:18, 20).

The hiss is a warning -- an alert that you are within a striking distance like a snake bite. It is similar to pointing a loaded weapon on the face of an intruder. Snakes warn before delivering their venom against trespassers. When a person is bitten by a venomous snake, they must rush quickly to a nearby hospital peradventure his or her life may be spared. It is no wonder when God hiss at a nation or kingdom, it draws a quick response because it's a prelude to a death strike. If you had stumbled upon a snake one time or another and you hear the hissing, it sets off a panic that tells you to hurry out of there before things go wrong. You only have a split-second decision to make because the venom is coming. The dosage is not the same with the early warning. You have the room to run for your life, however, if you chose to stay, you will pay a costly price. The hiss of the LORD is to cool off a hothead. Always, do not trespass means enter at your own risk! Imagine if the LORD God had given all authority and power to any of his created works. Imagine if one person could command every created thing on earth to use their weapons against a nation or kingdom and people. The LORD quickly removed Adam from the Garden of Eden when his life became exposed to the knowledge of good and evil. Knowledge is power and power is not dormant. Venom causes paralyses, which is part of incapacitating and disarming a daring opponent. Elements are still in the glory and no mistaken, they have great power. Adam was to subdue and rule over them because it takes a ruler to deal with rulers. The weapon of hiss creates sense of urgency to address impending urgent matters. When there is no more grace period, the hiss of the LORD is a panic button that wakes reluctant enemy to their senses -- to realize that time is up! **Calling upon the hiss of the LORD against the enemy is like sending venomous snakes into the chambers of the enemy. Some snake bites have no antidotes; therefore, they must run to the LORD immediately for negotiation to resolute the matter or perish. Nations or kingdoms know who has what weapons in their stockpiles!** You must shake the core and fabrics of your enemy with nerve rattling weapons of warfare. Some enemies are so stubborn that until death comes knowing at their doors, they will not show any remorse or regret.

EVENINGTIDE REBUKE - *And behold at eveningtide trouble; and before the morning he is not. This is the portion of them that spoil us, and the lot of them that rob us* (Isaiah 17:14).

Some weapons are very heart troubling: this programmable weapon is set for evening attack against the enemy. This weapon is released to create troubles in the evenings -- depriving the people rest or taking away the comforts of their daily accomplishments. When the people supposed to sit down and count their gains, they find everything empty like when a bank, a business or home is cleaned out by robbers. The spoilers quickly move out everything -- leaving the place empty. This surprising weapon is mean to the bone because it is aggravating the pain of reoccurring losses without the hope of solving the mysteries. Mystery losses are equivalent to mystery sicknesses and diseases -- you are at the mercy of your pain because every evening is yet another time of great loss and mourning. Eveningtide rebuke or trouble is fashioned to spoil the people -- the enemy by invading in the evening hour so that by tomorrow morning, everything is swept away without leaving any evidence of who is behind the attacks. It is a situation that will leave the enemy perplex and confused every day! **Program eveningtide rebuke of the LORD upon your enemy or territory to suffer reoccurring losses. The toll will subdue the enemy because there is no way to stop the mystery attacks or determine the culprit. The spirit realms are all about dealing with your enemy without leaving any traceable evidence. The Bible said, the secret things belong unto the LORD our God!** When you pull out certain weapon at your enemy, they will not hesitate to run for their lives. *At thy rebuke they fled; at the voice of thy thunder they hasted away* (Psalms 104:7).

FAN AND FANNERS - *Thou shalt fan them, and the wind shall carry them away, and the whirlwind shall scatter them: and thou shalt rejoice in the LORD, and shalt glory in the Holy One of Israel* (Isaiah 41:16).

And I will fan them with a fan in the gates of the land; I will bereave them of children, I will destroy my people, since they return not from their ways (Jeremiah 15:7).

FANNERS - *And will send unto Babylon fanners, that shall fan her, and shall empty her land: for in the day of trouble they shall be against her round about* (Jeremiah 51:2).

It is greatly mysterious to see how things work in the dimensions of the realms of God. The less suspected things are more dangerous than the things we tend to protect ourselves from. A fan is a tool for generating air and wind like wind-turbine or generator. A fanner is the asset trained to use the fan as a mechanical device. One thing that is mind-blowing about this concealed or hidden weapon is that it is used to scatter where the enemy or people have gathered. It is a weapon of ultimate confusion because it sends people into the spin around -- chasing after the wind for what is missing. It is a weapon that can make the enemy grievous because this weapon can be deployed to make unauthorized withdrawal from peoples' resources -- to cause sudden depletion and empty the storage room including bank accounts, food storage, armor depot and everything that people have built or what they are building for comfort and support. Fanners with their fans can secretly empty peoples' lives and storage shelves including disrupting their focus to achieve their ultimate goals or agendas. This is a cleanup weapon to sweep away peoples' safety nets. You see things where you put them a minute ago and suddenly, they are gone and you don't know how they managed to disappear without seeing anyone around. The wind generated from the weapon of fan by the fanners are destructive wind. It is to leave you with diminishing return by sucking away your assets and scatter them so you will not gather them back. You are literally working for nothing or saving into a broken bank all your life. This frightening weapon is used to attack nations or kingdoms' infrastructure to destabilize the security and destroy the advancement. The fanners with their fans can withdraw all the nations or kingdoms' resources and turn the place to desolation -- leaving the people broken in poverty and begging for life! It is an embargo and sanction weapon to blockade and stifle the progress of nations or kingdoms and people. **Whatever the enemy has stolen from you, deploy the armies of fanners with their fans to invade the territory or kingdom and strip the place of all your belongings including restitutions and punitive damages**! Inflict major confusion upon the life of your enemy by deploying this invisible weapon against your enemies. Ask the LORD to release them in Jesus name!

FISHERS AND HUNTERS - *Behold, I will send for many fishers, saith the LORD, and they shall fish them; and after will I send for many hunters, and they shall hunt them from* *every mountain, and from every hill, and out of the holes of the rocks* (Jeremiah 16:16).

The Lord GOD hath sworn by his holiness, that, lo, the days shall come upon you, that he will take you away with hooks, and your posterity with fishhooks (Amos 4:2).

Fishers of men are not only sent to save peoples' souls but also to bring their souls to judgment: death and destruction. Like bounty-hunters, hunters seek out people under judgment to execute the warrant of God's arrest with deadly force. Their behaviors are similar to hunting the wild animals so they are not sent to treat their targeted victims with tender care. The same way that fishermen throw their hook and baits, Fishers lure and snatch the souls of those whom they are sent to terminate. This is why the devils tempt their victims to do evil! They hook their souls to invade their bodies and they can also pull them out of their bodies to end their lives abruptly or untimely. Fishers and hunter are assassin squads or agents of the kingdom of heaven assigned to execute the orders of the LORD God upon people or the enemy. The human body contains a lot water and the environment and atmosphere are surrounded by water. The human life is like swimming in the ocean. The enemy also bait against peoples' souls to bring death and destruction upon them. This is to say that the enemy had learned the hidden secret from the glory. Fishers and hunters show unusual skills and expertise because they are trained and equipped to use their tools. Fishers and hunters are spiritual harvesters like those who harvest fruits from vineyards. They know how to operate under disguise as part of baiting against the enemy or victim. **Ask the LORD to send fishers and hunters against astral projected souls to snatch them in the spirit realms and bring them to the judgment of God. The witches and warlocks and wiccans or occultist are under the judgment of**

condemnation unless they repent and destroy their crafts! The Bible said, *Thou shalt not suffer a witch to live* (Exodus 22:18). Bring the judgment of God to their doors if they refuse to repent of their wickedness and atrocities! You must make them pay or they will keep playing!

FURY AND INDIGNATION - *But they rebelled against me, and would not hearken unto me: they did not every man cast away the abominations of their eyes, neither did they forsake the idols of Egypt: then I said, I will pour out my fury upon them, to accomplish my anger against them in the midst of the land of Egypt* (Ezekiel 20:8).

As silver is melted in the midst of the furnace, so shall ye be melted in the midst thereof; and ye shall know that I the LORD have poured out my fury upon you.

Therefore have I poured out mine indignation upon them; I have consumed them with the fire of my wrath: their own way have I recompensed upon their heads, saith the Lord GOD (Ezekiel 22:22, 31).

The boiling anger of the LORD God drives Him into rage and provokes his overwhelming response or action. This is more than any laser weapon or anything that produce light frequency or heatwave to achieve instant meltdown. The expression of the LORD in this stage of wrath is extremely dangerous because nothing is restraining Him. His grace and mercy, his love and compassion, his patience, longsuffering and temperance are all gone, and He is overtaking by rage and indignation to execute his vengeance. The indignation of the LORD is not what any enemy wants to see: no one wants to get on this side of Him because nothing will be left behind. To act in rage with immeasurable power is not a great idea even for the worst enemy. The cup of his indignation is somewhat a measured or calibrated response but to release the full indignation of the LORD is capping things off. Everything can be measured to some degree, nevertheless, there is always the fullness and the enemy never want anyone among the human race to ever bring down the depth of God that crushed and ended his attempted kingdom in heaven. (See Luke 1018; Revelation 12:7-9). As it is in heaven so also in the earth is a terrible news for the kingdom of satan and his demons including all the agents and agencies. The glory is the end of the kingdom rulership of satan whether in the spirit or physical realms. **Pray for the boiling anger of the LORD upon your enemy and provoke his indignation to respond with overwhelming force that will spare nothing! Bring an ultimate end to your enemy!** Gather intelligence on the evil of the enemy and report them to the LORD God and make them pay costly price!

RAVENOUS BIRDS - *No lion shall be there, nor any ravenous beast shall go up thereon, it shall not be found there; but the redeemed shall walk there* (Isaiah 35:9).

Thou shalt fall upon the mountains of Israel, thou, and all thy bands, and the people that is with thee: I will give thee unto the ravenous birds of every sort, and to the beasts of the field to be devoured (Ezekiel 39:4).

Ravens are clean-up crews -- like vultures they feast on the dead. Ravens do not like honorable burials! Their bellies are the tombs and graveyards of the unfortunate or the wicked. Ravens wait for the bodies of their victims to slump under the chokehold of the sting of death so they can celebrate with their flesh. Ravens do not mourn the dead because for them, it's an occasion to satisfy their drought. They ration the body parts of their victims --

denying the earth the power to retrieve the bodies for burial. Ravens are birds of prey! You cannot invite them to burial ceremonies: They will attack the living to claim the dead. The earth is part of concealing or securing the body of the deceased from the animals or agents that hunt the dead. When the enemy see birds of prey, they are discomforted because they know they are about to fall dead. Birds of prey have the senses to identify the dead among the living; therefore, they will pitch their tents and wait until the bodies begin to fall. Spiritually, people may not understand the significance or the implication of the sudden visit of the birds of prey. This is what people call evil birds but they are not only the animal species that prey on the victims of death. You just have to look in the spirit or everything would look normal. Birds of prey are harvesters of people's organs and when they are sent to attack their victims, they will begin to pick the body parts piece by piece. They are feeding on the victim while he or she is still trying to cling on to life. **When your enemy is stubborn and adaptive, you must send them the ravenous birds of preys to besiege his territory. Release them to feed on them alive and take away their parts until not a piece of their lives remain intact like Herod when the maggots stripped his body.** The wickedness of people is revealed upon death and vengeance begins with dishonoring their bodies. The earth can retain the body but the animals can also devour the bodies like Ahab and Jezebel. This is dishonorable discharge from this life! History is not kind to the wicked and evil! With Elijah the prophet of glory, the ravens brought him bread and flesh to sustain his life instead of waiting for him to fall dead. Always, God will turn evil for good!

NET - *My net also will I spread upon him, and he shall be taken in my snare: and I will bring him to Babylon to the land of the Chaldeans; yet shall he not see it, though he shall die there* (Ezekiel 12:13).

And I will spread my net upon him, and he shall be taken in my snare, and I will bring him to Babylon, and will plead with him there for his trespass that he hath trespassed against me (Ezekiel 17:20).

When they shall go, I will spread my net upon them; I will bring them down as the fowls of the heaven; I will chastise them, as their congregation hath heard (Hosea 7:12).

I was taken in the spirit to see how the enemy uses the nets to catch people in the spirit realms. The nets are spread across the pathways of unsuspecting victims, just like the fish nets but the nets are wider and bigger. Once the nets are setup, the enemy will begin to encompass the whole areas -- searching from different directions. As the person of interest is cornered or surrounded, the focus is to push him or her into the nets like a fish or animal. Unless the LORD opens your eyes to see in the spirit realms, weapons of nets are placed conspicuously because they blend into the environment so you will unsuspectedly walk right into it, and you are cut in the web. The weapon of nets is used to barricade, cut off areas to secure them for search and seizure or apprehension efforts. The enemy attempting to run away and escape will run right into the nets and fished out like a fish in the water or animals in the bush. Net is a weapon of entrapment to turn a person's life into endless struggle until the net is broken. Both humans and animals can be caught in the nets because the spirit realms have pathways! Therefore, anywhere pathways are created or retraceable can be mined, set traps and nets to catch whoever takes those pathways. **Ask the LORD to destroy the nets of the enemy. Command the nets of the enemy to catch those who cast them against you. Counter the enemy's net with the nets of the LORD. Destroy their nets by cutting holes on them or burning them up with the fire of God. You can also destroy the entire areas that the enemy is operating from.** The LORD is always your way of escape and He is there to rescue and deliver you in times of trouble.

FLYING ROLL - *Then I turned, and lifted up mine eyes, and looked, and behold a flying roll. And he said unto me, What seest thou? And I answered, I see a flying roll; the length thereof is twenty cubits, and the breadth thereof ten cubits. Then said he unto me, This is the curse that goeth forth over the face of the whole earth: for every one that stealeth shall be cut off as on this side according to it; and every one that sweareth shall be cut off as on that side according to it. I will bring it forth, saith the LORD of hosts, and it shall enter into the house of the thief, and into the house of him that sweareth falsely by my name: and it shall remain in the midst of his house, and shall consume it with the timber thereof and the stones thereof* (Zechariah 5:1-4).

The invisible realms are so powerful because of the mighty power of God. The way that events unfold in these dimensions are unparalleled to anything that humans can fathom. They are beyond what the human faculties could digest or even explain. The speed and agility of spiritual elements are incredibly potent. They are stealth so the radars of the human senses are not enough to detect them. They operate with impunity -- defying all security or defensive and protective measures. I have heard many people talk about entering the enemy's camp and taking back what the enemy has stolen from them.

First, the enemy's camp has a lot of defensive and offensive measures to repel and to retain aggressive opponent. You can be caught by the enemy so you need the help of the LORD. The enemy can aggressively repel and pursue after you. You need divine strategy: God's strategy comes with his weapons of attack and defense to assure your success and triumph. The LORD has ways to enforce his laws and cause his words to come to pass. He has weapons of war that are spiritually created to handle any dimension of warfare. When we know what to do and how to do them, there is assurance that we will see timely results. The weapon of flying roll is an airborne weapon designed to infiltrate the domain of thieves to inflict them with the curse of the LORD. The impact of this great weapon is to bring the judgment of God's curse that is attached to stealing. The Bible said, thou shall not steal! As long as the thieves continue to steal, the curses will continue multiply upon them. There is no way to deny as the means to escape the penalty of their crimes. When a thief is caught, he must pay back (return back what he has stolen) seven times plus applicable restitution or additional cost. Deploying this weapon into the houses of thieves is sowing the vengeance of curses upon them to force them to realize that stealing is not a hobby. Some missions are too risky to stick your neck out! Dimensional warfare is engaging a kingdom calibrated measures for complex warfare beyond what a person can do on his or her own. **Begin to pray and ask the LORD to deploy this weapon against any enemy that has been stealing from you. Let the curse of the LORD come upon them and make their lives and homes a living hell until they repent in ashes and dust. They must return your stuffs or they will continue to pay a dear price!**

RODS BECAME SERPENTS - Exodus 7:12: *For they cast down every man his rod and they became serpents; but*

Aaron's rod swallowed up their rods.

The power of creation is used to transform or convert the physical material to spiritual equivalence and the spiritual to physical equivalence, respectively. The phenomena are parts of concealing all things in the glory. The elements of surprises abound in the glory because of the wonders of God. The LORD God multiplies and increases His wonders innumerably to captivate and punish until you are humbled before Him. Although wonders are to arouse your suspicion and detain your spiritual focus, because you are not able to comprehend the depth of the revelation, you are bound to become confused like Pharaoh. The revelation of God is the way to save you from getting swept away! Wonders are close-encounters before the appearing of the LORD God. If you fail to yield the right of way, the glory of God will consume you. Wonders are the last dimensions to change your mindset before you meet your judgment. Testimonials of elements in the glory are self-sacrifices and legal statements before the throne of God because they are risking their lives without perjuring themselves. Secondly, the LORD God is enthroned – in other word, the appearing of His glory is the appearing of His throne of judgment. The revelation of the throne of His judgment is releasing His rulership decrees and authorizing the Hosts of Heavens and all the created works to respond according to His judgment. A broomstick is enough to kill and destroy in the glory. This is why He puts a mark on people to spare them from destruction by the elements. The glory disarms all things by taking away their lives, authority and power; therefore, the dead cannot fight warfare and it is why vengeance belong unto the LORD God! Making everything to disappear in the glory is cleaning up the enemy's mess. The enemy you see today, you shall see them no more! **Ask for great signs and wonders: Acts 5:12 said, "Now by the hands of the apostles (special** messengers) numerous and startling signs and wonders were being performed among the people."

WATER TRANSFORMED TO BLOOD - Exodus 7:17: *Thus says the Lord, In this you shall know, recognize, and understand that I am the Lord: behold, I will smite with the rod in my hand the waters in the [Nile] River, and they shall be turned to blood. The fish in the river shall die, the river shall become foul smelling, and the Egyptians shall loathe to drink from it.*

A location or base can go through makeovers. Part of battle strategies is camouflage! An environment can go through change and an atmosphere can experience a sudden transformation. Behold I make all things new! The impacts of change and transformation are to create unfamiliarity. Taking away the consciousness of the old is to destroy the awareness of the present to affect the hope of the future. The new is often harder to adjust to. Momentary shift destroys the comfort of familiarity -- it is like throwing a monkey-wrench into a known formula. It is taken the season and time backwards! The works of familiar spirits are to acquaint or become familiarized with people, a person, a thing and a place. This is why devils work through the systems of the world, the societies, cultures and traditions of the people. All demonic assignments are divided into two important area of life: 1) geographically and 2) demographically. Impacting a geographic location or a people's group is redrawing the map spiritually and physically. Some changes and transformation cannot be quickly reversed so they are permanent! The reason we need the great power of God is to impact the lives of the people, the environment and the atmosphere simultaneously. We want every sphere of life to be affected: the waterways, the land-spaces, the airspaces, the elements, the animals, humans and spirits, etc. You must take away the ability of the enemy to maintain familiarity with your environment, atmosphere, family, yourself and children. People move from one place or location to another hoping that their problems will go away, only to walk right into the same problem or inherit more problems. You must redraw the map by impacting change and transformation upon your environment and atmosphere by the authority and power of God. Spiritual maps are redrawn by change and transformation! Familiarity is part of gaining advantage through mastership: You rule by maintaining a routine around the people's lives and places -- to keep everything working the same way. Change and transformation forces everything to shift into a different mode so things are no longer the same way they were before. Routine path of life is a gateway to bondage and captivity! The enemy does not have to work extremely hard to understand how things really operate. It is a giveaway because the enemy can simply blend into the system and ride the momentum forever. Our lives are not the only thing that experience change and transformation when the great power of God invades, our environment and atmosphere experience a great shift and it's the key to dislodging powers that are embedded in those locations. Taking away authority and power from the enemy is not limited to binding the enemy but denying the enemy access and accessibility to utilize different geographic locations and affecting the demography. By redrawing the map spiritually and physically, you cut down on the enemies' advancement and stifle their operations. You will dwarf their activities and set them back for years -- allowing for the people to escape. All things must work together for our good according to God's divine purpose. **Command the elements, the land, the air, the people, the animals, the water -- every created thing to declare the glory of God. Apply the blood of Jesus over your territory and jurisdiction, over your environment and your atmosphere to declare the redemption of the LORD! Bring the kingdom**

rulership of the LORD God over them to subject them under his great authority and power! *The heavens declare the glory and the earth showed his handiwork* (Psalms 19:1). *The earth is the LORD's and the fullness thereof; the world, and they that dwell in therein. For He hath founded it upon the seas, and established it upon the floods* (Psalms 24:1-2).

All created works of God are military reservists and they can be called up for battles. It does not matter if they are only insects. Some are serving in active duties and some are waiting for orders or call of duty. If they are armed for the battles of the LORD, they are there to assistant you in dimensional warfare because God's purpose and destiny for your life are at stake. Everything that serve the purpose of God must grant you access to God's destiny or destination for your life. There is no destiny without a destination! Ask the LORD God to release them to collaborate with you in battles. Remember that He is the LORD of Hosts and Captain of the Hosts; therefore, it's not praying randomly but operating according to the dynamics of his strategies. Here are more epic weapons for you:

FROGS WERE CALLED INTO BATTLE - Exodus 8:5: *And the Lord said to Moses, Say to Aaron, Stretch out your hand with your rod over the rivers, the streams and canals, and over the pools, and cause frogs to come up on the land of Egypt.*

GNATS WERE CALLED UP - Exodus 8:16: *The Lord said to Moses, Say to Aaron, Stretch out your rod and strike the dust of the ground, that it may become biting gnats or mosquitoes throughout all the land of Egypt.*

GADFLIES JOINED THE ARMIES - Exodus 8:21: *behold,*

I will send swarms [of bloodsucking gadflies] upon you, your servants, and your people, and into your houses; and the houses of the Egyptians shall be full of swarms [of blood-sucking gadflies], and also the ground on which they stand.

LIVESTOCKS WERE TARGETED AND DESTROYED - Exodus 9:3: *Behold, the hand of the Lord [will fall] upon your livestock which are out in the field, upon the horses, the donkeys, the damsels, the herds and the flocks; there shall be a very severe plague.*

HAIL WAS USED - Exodus 9:23: *Then Moses stretched forth his rod toward the heavens, and the Lord sent thunder and hail, and fire (lightning) ran down to and along the ground, and the Lord rained hail upon the land of Egypt.*

LOCUSTS WAS CALLED –Exodus 10:12: *Then the Lord said to Moses, Stretch out your hand over the land of Egypt for the locusts, that they may come up on the land of Egypt and eat all the vegetation of the land, all that the hail has left.*

DARKNESS WAS USED AS WEAPON OF WAR - Exodus 10:21: *And the Lord said to Moses, Stretch out your hand toward the heavens, that there may be darkness over the land of Egypt, a darkness which may be felt.*

We see that in Egypt the LORD blanketed the land with thick darkness or fullness of darkness without allowing any transparency so they could see themselves. They were buried in obscurity and the land was paralyzed: the mobility of the people was seized including animals, etc. Spiritual calendars of events are regulated or scheduled by the order of the luminaries – the rising of the sun and the going down. Seasons and time also play pivotal roles as well as seconds, minutes, hours, days weeks, months, yeas and ages. Touching these orders of life is stifling the enemy's momentum. Joshua took out the handover of the orders of creation to limit the transition of day and night and his enemies could not escape into the deep darkness of the night. The empire of Pharaoh saw the weapon of darkness that paralyzed the kingdom – devastating the economy and discomforting the people and the land in general! **Blanket the enemy's territories or domains with thick darkness that they will not see themselves. Incapacitate their mobility by freezing up their assets and cut off their lifelines. Speak to darkness to cover the enemy territories or domains and cover their eyes to blind their sights while stagnating their efforts to rise or advance! Stop the day from giving them light.** Darkness is what retires the day to take over the shift so everyone has to wait for another day. Like Elijah your fervent pray under the compelling zeal of the LORD will devastate your enemy in ways you may have never thought possible or humanly envisioned.

FIRSTBORN OF THE LAND WERE TARGETED - Exodus 11:4: *And Moses said, 'Thus says the Lord, About midnight I will go out into the midst of Egypt; and all the first born in the land [the pride, hope and joy] of Egypt shall die, from the firstborn of Pharaoh, who sits on his throne, even to the firstborn of the maidservant who is behind the hand mill, and all the firstborn of beasts.*

Death is the human's greatest paranoia and worst tragedy – they are willing to forfeit everything or give up whatever they have to save their lives. Satan as adversary know this deep secret (Job 2:4). Losing a loved one or losing any life to death is generally grievous. When the angel of death – spiritual assassins invaded the kingdom of Egypt and killed their priced first sons, the devil could not convince the kingdom of Egypt to keep the people of

Israel in captivity and bondage. Secondly, impacting the kingdom rulership of satan by targeting the governmental or other agencies that are established upon satanic order of rulership, is cutting back satan's kingdom system. The kingdom of satan needs a lifeline – to remain connected to the world systems: government, economy, technology, religious, societies, customs and traditions, holidays and other events, etc. People can suffer great loss of everything including their lives as you use this mighty weapon of mass destruction. **Ask the LORD God to release the angels of death upon your stubborn enemies and cripple their hope for life including targeting their own lives. Subject their whole kingdom spiritually and physically to painful consequences by releasing death upon the land!** Death multiplies mourning and grief upon the people and strip away their moral courage for battle! The pain of war falls upon a nation or kingdom and people. There is a shared distribution of the suffering depending on the casualties!

PILLAR OF CLOUD AND FIRE - Exodus 14:19-20: *And the Angel of God Who went before the host of Israel moved and went behind them; and the pillar of the cloud went from before them and stood behind them, coming between the host of Egypt and the host of Israel. It was as cloud and darkness to the Egyptians, but it gave light by night to the Israelites; and the one host did not come near the other all night.*

Ezekiel 39:6: *I will send fire on Magog and upon those who dwell securely in the coast lands, and they shall know, understand, and realize that I am the Lord [the Sovereign Ruler, Who calls forth loyalty and obedient service].*

The pillar of cloud and fire are parts of the revelation of the majestic glory of God. They are heavenly backup supports to stop the enemy's advancement while propelling the people God. You cannot pass through these barriers without being consumed or subjected to death. Never forget that the glory is a defense. (See Isaiah 4:5; Zechariah

2:5). Ascension into the realms of God takes spiritual certification so you cannot not just walk through the glory defense. The Garden of Eden was protected by the
Archangel Cherubim with flaming swords. The majestic
glory is engaging the created works of God with extraordinary power to execute his judgment decrees. Therefore,
they have full authorization and power to kill and destroy.
The glory is a defense -- to secure and protect kingdom
interest besides fulfilling kingdom purposes. The majestic
glory is potently devastating in warfare. Any time the
LORD God uses the elements for warfare, everything is
destroyed. **Call for the elements of God's creation to
respond vigorously according to the purpose of God
for your life.** Elements in the glory know the secrets of
the glory and understand not to trespass when they see
the security defense of the glory of the LORD God. They
also know the voice of the LORD God. Any time the humans take the risk to venture in or intrude, they perish!
(See Exodus 14:23-28; Job 1:9-10a).

THE SEA WAS DIVIDED TO CREATE A PASSAGE
WAY - Exodus 14:21-22: *Then Moses stretched out his
hand over the sea, and the Lord caused the sea to go
back by a strong east wind all that night and made the sea
dry land; and the waters were divided. And the Israelites
went into the midst of the sea on dry ground, the waters
being a wall to them on their right hand and on their left.*

When you hear about the baptism of death, it's a warning
not to trespass! In the realms of God passages are
granted by the rulership authority and power because it is
safeguarding the kingdom entry point and agendas. You
can lose your life by advancing beyond the point of re-
striction unless you are given the passage to cross. Any
time the river, the lake, the sea and ocean cross their
thresholds, it means entering a new dimension. Dimensional warfare is using everything available to the kingdom to enforce the rulership orders of the king. There is
no limit to dimensional warfare because it is opening the
gates of abyss, hell, depth, width, length and height –
everything it will take to conquer and overcome or subdue
and rule. Depth, length, width and height are weapons of
escalation: you can lose your life by venturing into a place
you are not supposed to go. **Take your enemies
through dangerous spiritual and physical terrains by
pulling down the supernatural power of God to ex-
haust their abilities to withstand. Force them to pursue after you right into the great judgment of God so
they will never rise again.**

THE ENEMY ADVANCING GUN BOATS AND SHIPS WERE CUT OFF - JOSHUA 3:16: *Then the waters which came down from above stood and rose UP IN A HEAP far off, at Adam, the city that is beside Zarenthan; and those FLOWING DOWN toward the Sea of the Arabah, the Salt [Dead] Sea, were wholly cut off. And the people passed over opposite Jericho.*

There is no way to touch the realms of dimensional warfare without experiencing the unthinkable and unimaginable. There are spiritual intercepts and intelligence gathering besides engaging in warfare! The purpose of God will not fail and the words that came out of his mouth are judgment decrees – they will not return void or fail. The intervention of heaven cannot be challenged whether the people of God are using cooking knives or sling shots. Everything is super-imposed and the abilities are spiritually altered. Elements are created for epic spiritual warfare but we can begin to network with them only by God's orders because of their immense power. They are restricted and controlled by the LORD of Hosts and the Captain of the Hosts. We need the order of the LORD to release their powers to work against the enemy. Elements are rulers over their domains and they can cut off the enemies' passage ways and end their abilities to keep fighting. Extreme weather condition can cut off a whole nation or kingdom. In the glory it's all about increase and multiplication whether through unification of all things to operate as one, or creating and activating great numbers of armies momentarily. Both the strength and numbers can increase and multiply to overwhelm any enemy! Send elements to intervene approaching enemy armies against your life. Destroy their weapons if they advance beyond the point of restrictions. Stubborn enemies die stubborn deaths. Engage the realms of God to unleash epic weapons of dimensional warfare in the glory!

THE RIVER WAS DIVIDED TO CREATE A PASSAGE WAY - Joshua 3:17: *And while ALL Israel passed over on dry ground, the priests who bore the ark of the covenant of the Lord stood firm ON DRY GROUND in the midst of the Jordan, until ALL the nation finished passing over the Jordan.*

The Ark of the Covenant represented the manifested presence of God. Real authentic anointing can produce degrees of the miraculous signs. The anointing destroys the yoke and removes the burden. (See Isaiah 10:27). The people of God can go beyond the enemy defense line but it all depends on the level and measure of God's presence and power on their lives. Most importantly, the anointing is for work and levels of warfare – especially personal and territorial warfare. **You must seriously ask the LORD God to anoint you with the Holy Spirit and with power.** The anointing is used to enhance the instrument of war; therefore, the instrument of the anointing and the anointed are combined or united in the workforce: labor and warfare to achieve true victory and break-throughs. The reason is that the Holy Spirit is not only the Spirit of Might but also the Spirit of Knowledge, Under-standing, Wisdom, Counsel, Fear of the LORD and Judg-ment. There are disadvantages to fighting with the anointing so you must carefully follow the leadership of the Holy Spirit to avoid sabotaging your personal security.

THE SUN IMPACTED TO GIVE EXTRA DAY - Joshua 10:13: *And the sun stood still, and the moon stayed, until the nation took vengeance upon their enemies. Is not this written in the Book of Jasher? So the sun stood still in the midst of the heavens and did not hasten to go down for about a whole day.*

The heavens declare the glory – the elements declaring the glory is losing their lives or stopping at nothing to fulfill God's order of rulership decrees without contempt. This is why the LORD God trust them with extraordinary power because they will not sabotage the operations. They will not take the glory – honor and worship of the LORD God. Declaring the glory is to act verbatim according to divine orders without adding or removing, which is loyalty and faithfulness. **You must pray and ask the LORD God to authorize the elements of his created works to coop-erate – collaborate and corroborate with you in ful-filling you purpose and destiny for the glory of God.** The networking of the elements and the people of God are parts of fulfilling the role of the first Adam – to get all things to work together according to God's purpose for his life! Dominion is synchronizing all created things including the humans to accomplish the purpose of God without allowing any outside interruption, interference and interception!

THE SEA SWALLOWED ENEMY - Exodus 14:28: *The waters returned and covered the chariots, the horsemen, and all the host of Pharaoh that pursued them; not even one of them remained. But the Israelites walked on dry ground in the midst of the sea, the waters being a wall to them on their right hand and on their left.*

The execution of judgment is precisely carrying out whatever is decreed. In that case, there is no obligation or repercussion on the part of the enforcement agent and agency. They are doing their jobs or fulfilling their purpose. It is the reason you do not incur retaliation or retribution in the glory! You have to remember that the kingdom of heaven carries out order of arrests – to bind and loose, prosecute, sentence, kill and destroy! Commanding the elements to respond according to the order of God's judgment is inflicting the enemy with immeasurable pain. No enemy whether, angel, human, devil, animal and element want to fight the glory of God! Operating according to divine purpose is one of the greatest problems of the enemy because the purpose of God cannot fail. (See Isaiah 14:24; 55:11). **Pray for the LORD God to introduce you to the elements of His created works like the First Adam and the Second Adam.** This is part of operating in dominion or ruling with Christ in God!

CLOUD BY DAY AND FIRE BY NIGHT - Exodus 13:21: *The Lord went before them by day in a pillar of cloud to lead them along the way and by night in a pillar of fire to give them light, that they might travel by day and by night.*

When the clouds form, the rain usually follow immediately even as fire produces excess heat or destroy everything on its path. Cloud is also insulation or covering -- a hide away: it depicts the durst of God's feet so it's a strong support. Fire on the other hand is element of change to create a different form. Revealing the glory of the LORD God over the elements is to produce His attributes over the created works. In other word, the behaviors of the elements are not mere camouflage. They are covered with weapons of unparalleled power! The glory consumes, overshadows, and conceals – not just as a defense but also to engage offensively. Therefore, when you begin to engage the elements of God's created works, it is part of invoking overwhelming force to destroy the existence of the enemy. Everything that is created in the glory is for epic warfare and they do not lose their strength! You can outpace your enemy as these elements work as security details and entourages around your life! The angels are not the only ones that encamp round about you to help you with warfare or protect your life from dangers!

MEAT AND BREAD FROM HEAVEN - Exodus 16:13: *In the evening quails came up and covered the camp; and in the morning the dew lay round about the camp. And when the dew had gone, behold, upon the face of the wilderness there lay a fine, round and flake like thing, as fine as hoarfrost on the ground.* (It was manna.)

Part of the suffering of war is draught, famine, pestilence, injuries, wounds and deaths. The blockade of the enemy to starve and force the opponents to surrender is not to be underestimated. The game of war is using every tactic to defeat your enemy. In some cases, it is not all about carrying the big guns. Having access when all access is denied or cut off is part of surviving the horrors of war. The Bible said, He shall supply all your needs according to His riches in glory through Christ Jesus. (See Philippians 4:19). The law of supply is to instigate and perpetuate continuous delivery and the battlefields and battlefronts are not exempt. **In your seasons of warfare, never forget to ask the LORD for miraculous delivery of heaven blessings upon your life.** You will endure better through the seasons until you defeat or conquer and overcome your enemies or pass your test.

THE GROUND OPENED AND SWALLOWED THE ENEMY - Numbers 16:31: *As soon as Moses stopped speaking, the ground under the offenders split apart and the earth opened its mouth and swallowed them and their households and [Korah and] all [his] men and all their possessions.*

When we say that the glory affects the atmosphere, it means that revelation impacts the order of creation because it is how the created work came to being. They were not only called to being but created materially and immaterially by the great power of the LORD God.

Revelation is the opening of the hidden hatches of the compartment of life and living things. All created works have secrets about their lives that until the secrets are revealed, the mysteries will remain hidden. Revelation touches the secrets of purpose to bring out a different character or ability that is not generally and openly expressed. To see the Earth open the hidden compartment to execute the order of God's decree was something unfathomable. There are secrets of the LORD that are overwhelmingly mind-blowing and the compelling power establishes the great trembling fear of the LORD God. Having great authority and power with the LORD goes beyond touching other people's lives to affecting the order of creation. The creation is part of upholding the kingdom rulership of God; therefore, their cooperation is extremely important. Without their collaboration and corroboration, the network will be broken. Great authority and power come with great intelligence or secrets and when the keys are released, the impact is enormous. There is urgent advancement which cannot wait and securing the passage calls for mandatory compliance and it is why the purpose of God is prioritized! **Speak to the elements of God's created works to respond and grant you access and accessibility to your destination to fulfill the purpose of God for your life. Release them by the word of the LORD to punish opposing powers and stop them from any interruption or hindrance.**

DISEASES WERE WEAPONIZED - Exodus 9:8: *The Lord said to Moses and Aaron, Take handfuls of ashes or soot from the brick kiln and let Moses sprinkle them toward the heavens in the sight of Pharaoh. 9/ And it shall become small dust over all the land of Egypt, and become boils* *breaking out in sores on man and beast in all the land [occupied by the Egyptians].*

Numbers 16:41, 44, 45, 49: *But on the morrow all the congregation of the Israelites murmured against Moses and Aaron, saying, 'You have killed the people of the Lord.' And the Lord said to Moses, 'Get away from among this congregation, that I may consume them in a moment.' And Moses and Aaron fell on their faces. Now those who died in the plague were 14,700, besides those who died in the matter of Korah.*

Plagues are strange sicknesses and diseases: they are often incurable by physicians. Always, know that the spirit realms are concealed and whatever they are doing are in the secrets. Therefore, whatever weapon of attack they use to afflict and inflict people may not quickly yield or provide the remedial cure to reverse the impact. This is why they can last for long and in many cases, the powers behind the incidents may have to be appealed to, and appeased to withdraw or stop their strange attacks. The Bible said, there is nothing hidden that shall not be revealed. In the world, the militaries research and develop chemical and biological weapons which includes manufacturing airborne diseases besides chemical agents. This is to say that plagues – sicknesses and diseases can be weaponized in battles. We see Egypt being hit with plagues – impacting animals and human lives. Another damaging part is that the plagues can be formulated to engage and target specific areas of life. Strange sicknesses and diseases can bring strange impact on people – rendering them impotent. Taking away the soldiers' ability to fight is winning without having to fight. You want to force your enemy to retire prematurely. Surprise attack can only be achieved with surprise weapon of attack!

Don't think that it is easy to bring a nation or kingdom to surrender or negotiating table without elements of surprises. As long as they have immunity, there can be no diplomacy, bipartisan, collateral or bilateral agreements. **Plague your enemy with severe sickness and disease – spiritual chemical and biological weapons to destroy them with toxicity. Bring strange pestilence – airborne diseases and terminal sicknesses upon them until their history is blotted out of the earth. Ask the LORD God to open the heavenly laboratory and release the agents of death to wipe out the enemy population so they will rise no more.** This is why no enemy wants to fight the glory of God! The Bible said, *the enemy fear and tremble*! (See James 2:19). Astral projection shows that the enemy can intrude inside people's lives, and astral travel show that the enemy can infiltrate different places whether familiar or otherwise. Now, you have to know that they can also be caught, arrested and prosecuted or punished for their illegal crimes even if they shape-shifted to take on different forms and looks or appearances. Their objects or subjects of disguises can be investigated and incriminated. The tools can be seized and destroyed and their identities can be exposed like in the cases of busting spy rings. And besides, the secret evidences can be extracted and used against them in judgment. The Bible said, *So the LORD sent pestilence upon Israel: and there fell of Israel seventy thousand men* (1 Chronicles 21:14). *For thus saith the Lord GOD; How much more when I send my four sore judgments upon Jerusalem, the sword, and the famine, and the noisome beast, and the pestilence, to cut off from it man and beast?* (Ezekiel 14:21).

ENGAGE THE POWER OF SPIRITUAL SUPPLIES:

WATER CAME FROM A ROCK - Numbers 20:11: *And Moses lifted up his hand and with his rod he smote the rock twice. And the water came out abundantly, and the congregation drank, and their livestock.*

RAVENS BROUGHT BREAD AND MEAT - I Kings 17:6: *And the ravens brought him bread and flesh in the morning and bread and flesh in the evening, and he drank of the brook.*

FOOD DID NOT RUN OUT - 1 Kings 17:14: *For thus says the Lord, the God of Israel: The jar of meal shall not waste away or the bottle of oil fail until the day that the Lord sends rain on the earth.*

The deeper realms of God are where nothing is impossible because of God's greater personal engagement. A supernatural life is not contingent to external provisions. Some of us may not understand that water is not the only thing the rock can produce by the creative power of God. When David as a young boy took on the battle of the nation of Israel, he defeated Goliath with stones and a slingshot. Your prayers can shed the rocks out of mountains and turn the pieces of the rocks into weapons to drive and chase away powerful armies. I have personally seen these things in the spirit realms. There are concealed weapons as there are open carry! In the realms of God, you will deal with concealed weapons of incredible power. **The created works are not only weaponized, they can also use their weapons to help you to achieve the purpose of God.** We are in a time that elements will respond to the sons of God like in the days of Moses, Joshua and Elijah. Spiritual supplies and provisions are not limited to foods and drinks but also weapons of warfare!

RAIN WAS STOPPED - I Kings 17:1: *Elijah the Tishbite, of the temporary residents of Gilead, said to Ahab, As the Lord, the God of Israel, lives, before Whom I stand, there shall not be dew or rain these years but according to My word.*

You can sanction or place embargoes on your enemy or choke off a whole territory and lock down a domain. The vast areas of dimensional warfare cover many parts that only few people have uncovered. Successful warfare takes more than one kind of weapon of war. This is why nations or kingdoms stockpile different weapons in the case of war scenarios. Cutting of the rain is drying up the enemy's harvest of war spoils. It is taking away bread from their mouths to reduce their surplus until they beg for bread. Warfare and famine are not compatible. Water is part of life – the human body is full of water even as the soil or earth is full of water. Above the earth is full of water. The nourishment and replenishment of human supplies depend on enough water supply. When water is taken out of the earth, it needs a replenishment and likewise the human body. Water spirits need water and when their waters are dried up; they languish in despair. Turn their waters into deserts and increase the heatwaves over the deserts to turn it into burning hell. **Dry up the enemy waters, place embargos and sanctions on them by cutting of God's blessing from raining on them.** God rains upon the righteous and the wicked and evil. Take away their comforts by depleting their lifelines! Elijah was a man of like passion and through his prayer, he cut off the rain from a whole nation and people. Discomforting the agents and agencies that the enemy use is part of disrupting his evil agendas and crippling their efforts to advance!

THE DEAD RAISED UP TO LIFE - 1 Kings 17:21: *And he stretched himself upon the child three times and cried to the Lord and said, O Lord my God, I pray You, let this child's soul come back into him.* (It did!)

When you are fighting the enemy in the spirit realms, you must watch out. Life and power are given instantly, which is to say that even objects can become delicate weapons like the jawbone of a donkey. The glory realms are full of death and life scenarios: things are suspended in motions like remote control pause. This is because of the full control of life to suspend and release – *be still and know that I AM God.* (See Psalms 46:10). When everything look like there is no life anywhere or vacuum, you must proceed cautiously. Trespassing into the spirit realms is extremely dangerous! It is why you are transformed wholly to enter the spirit realms because it takes a whole you to live fully in the spiritual dimensions or you will become immediate causality. In the physical life nations or kingdoms issue constant warnings as precautions to protect the lives of their citizens. The spirit realm is hostile and brutally aggressive so you must accelerate and function like the LORD God or you stand no chance. In His image after His likeness is to achieve important spiritual conformity. God does not want us to meddle in spiritual things in ignorance because it's a one-way ticket to self-destruction. The spirit realms are full of decoys and proxies – the confusion is too great to a point that without unusual transparency and clarity, no created works of God will know Him or worship Him. Resurrection of the death is part of personal representation to avoid given away the key of defense to impostors or the spirit of death. This is why God is not the God of the dead! **Pray for the LORD God to raise up everything that is dead in your life and bring exceptional spiritual transparency and clarity in your life to operate fully in the spirit realms as well as in the physical realm – as it is in heaven so also in the earth!**

FIRE CAME FROM THE LORD - 1 Kings 18:38: *Then the fire of the Lord fell and consumed the burnt sacrifice and the wood and the stones and the dust, and also licked up the water that was in the trench.*

For our God is a consuming fire (Deuteronomy 4:24; Hebrews 12:29).

Answering by fire is one of the spiritual phenomena. You must know that the created works of God are living expression of Him. They speak His language because the LORD God is the author of the languages. They are used as choreographic instruments to coordinate the appearing of the LORD God. When you call on the LORD, He can answer through the elements. Phenomena are parts of spiritual revelation – they are careful depiction of the wonders of God. Some of the great secrets of the wonders of God is that the elements that typify or symbolize His manifestation and revelation are used as attributes of God. The Heavens declare the glory and the Earth show His handiwork – they are speaking expressively and demonstratively as actor agents and representatives. And their actions are not impulsive but faithful and loyal obedience to orders. This is why they are trusted and used to declare the glory. Their obedience is equivalence to the LORD God appearing personally to do things. They are doing what He commands them to do in answers to your prayers. **Ask the LORD to open your eyes to see how He uses His majestic glory to defense against His purpose. You will begin to call down fire to consume your enemy and summon other elements of His created works in your battles.**

RAIN CAME DOWN - 1 Kings 18:41: *And Elijah said to Ahab, Go up, eat and drink, for there is the sound of abundance of rain.*

Restoration is bringing back what was lost, taken away, confiscated, stolen, misplaced, revoked including access and accessibility. Our authority and power are enormous in God, we only have to engage in this dimension to experience the reality. No nation or kingdom and people including the enemy is immune or exempt from the law of God or excluded from obeying the voice of the LORD God. The people of God who represent his kingdom interest can operate in great authority and power of God. The blessings of God are incentives bestowed upon the people when they cooperate with the LORD God. **When the people reject the counsel of God, the people of God can call for the judgment of God to withhold the incentives – impacting everyone involved in the rebellion whether it relates to a person, a nation state or a kingdom spiritually and physically.** You must attack their schedules and destroy their assignments. Delete their calendars and erase their programming. This is how righteousness is enforced and the wicked is brought down by stopping their agendas and destroying their works.

ELIJAH RAN TWENTY MILES - 1 Kings 18:46: *The hand of the Lord was on Elijah. He girded up his loins and ran before Ahab to the entrance of Jezreel [nearly twenty miles].*

Spiritual acceleration is to cut down on fatigue, exhaustion and weakness. This is the way your enemy cannot overtake you or escape from you. The spirit realm takes great speed because of ascension and revelation besides the power of creation and the power of resurrection. Though they were dead yet shall they live again – often, suddenly because of the spirit entering into them. Angels excel in strength besides the Holy Spirit is the Spirit of life and the power of the Highest! (See Psalms 103:20-21; Luke 1:35; Romans 8:2). It is part of concealing all things in the glory to operate whether alive or dead by releasing instant life and power. Acceleration is to expedite and cover immeasurable distance without the constraint of barriers whether spiritually or physically. If you are going to excel in the spirit realms, you need the fullness of the life and extraordinary power of the LORD God, which takes relinquishing your own life to Him. The spirit realm is like a womb and it is the reason why you experience whole transformation. You are either born or created so the process of completion is accelerated and expedited. Don't let your enemy escape into the secret compartments of the spirit realms and hide themselves away. Find them and expose them and let them pay for what they have done against you. **Release your life wholly to God so the Spirit of the LORD God will translate you into the spirit realms or angels and elements will carry you and take you into the spirit realms**

quickly and show you where they are hiding.

ANIMALS ATTACKED THE ENEMY - 2 Kings 2:24: *And he turned around and looked at them and called a curse down on them in the name of the Lord. And two she-bears came out of the woods and ripped up forty-two of the boys.*

Everything is weaponized in the spirit realms and the enemy understands the concept much better than many people of God. The reason is that they know the glory! The glory is a defense! In a nutshell, the created works are used to enforce the order of God's judgment decree and they are greatly equipped or empowered for epic warfare. Therefore, the enemy steals their images or identities and simulate their behavioral characteristics and fighting skills to use in warfare. In the martial art, you will see how different spirits using animal behaviors can be summoned or invoke to enter into people's body to learn their technical skills. It is common for people to find themselves fighting with different creatures in the spirit realms. Everything that is created is for the purpose of God so its normal for the enemy to mimic their looks and behaviors to deceive. Nevertheless, by their fruit ye shall know them because the thief come to steal, kill and destroy. You must **destroy all the devised weapons of the enemy including all duplications, simulations and reverse engineering of God's created works. Jesus was manifested to destroy the works of the devils. Command the elements that the enemies are using their images, forms, behaviors and skills to be destroyed. Release fire into the mechanisms and apparatus, and force the devils or astral projected souls to come out of the elements. Bind the evil powers that are using the**

elements for warfare. Loose God's animals against their animals to destroy them like the case of Moses and pharaoh. Another important thing about the glory is the unification of all things as one with the LORD God. The enemy wants to blend his life into other created works of God and use them as gateways to do his evil works. These are hidden strategies of dimensional spiritual warfare! *I will meet them as a bear that is bereaved of her whelps, and will rend the caul of their heart, and there will I devour them like a lion: the wild beast shall tear them* (Hosea 13:8).

RECOVER LOST WEAPONS OR TOOLS - 2 Kings 6:5-6: *But as one was felling his beam, the ax head fell into the water; The man of God said, Where did it fall? When shown the place, Elisha cut off a stick and threw it in there, and THE IRON FLOATED.*

Spiritual weapons are often concealed; therefore, losing your weapons does not mean that you cannot recover or retrieve them. This is why you must know and understand how spiritual warfare really work. The retrieval mechanism takes engaging the LORD: you need the manifestation of the presence of the Holy Spirit and the revelation of the LORD God. The LORD can teach you inspirationally by His Spirit but He can also reveal secret weapons to you in the intense heat of warfare. If you understand the manifested presence and the revelation of God, everything will become much easier for you to access in the realms of the spirit. Remember that as its in Heaven (spirit) so also in the Earth (physical). The presence of the Holy Spirit is what turns the created works into weapons of war by enhancing or transforming them to fit into divine purpose of God. The battlefield and battlefront are wherever these weapons suddenly become alive – spiritually, physically and otherwise, so be on the lookout for conspicuous stashes of unusual weapons in the spirit realms. They often appear as a way to release them to you! These are the ways that the LORD hides them and leads you to where they are or suddenly open them up to you. **Ask the LORD God to lead you to your hidden weapons or show you where they are stored up so you can access them momentarily!** Spirit, soul and body are parts of dimensions; therefore, achieving the unification as one is the key to realizing the full potential. This is why the glory unify all things with the LORD God so that the fullness of God's life and great power can be exerted over their lives to achieve the impossible. For with God nothing shall be impossible!

GATHER INTELLIGENCE ON YOUR ENEMY - 2 Kings 6:12: *One of his servants said, None, my lord O king; but Elisha, the prophet who is in Israel, tells the king of Israel the words that you SPEAK IN YOUR BEDCHAMBER.*

Often, we don't understand why nations or kingdoms maintain different intelligence apparatus. Authority and power can only be as effective as the intelligence capacity. False intelligence is equivalent to blind-spot and in the event of critical decision, you will lack clear directive. There must be a pointed and exit strategies in spiritual warfare or you will walk right into endless confusion. You must have the capacity to gather intelligence on your enemy to know where they are and where to attack. Warfare is not something you must engage in ignorance. The Bible said, you must not be ignorant of satan's devices: His weapons, strategic approaches, maneuverability and other hidden measures. The spirit realms are dangerous blind-spots to the natural man. (See 1 Corinthians 2:14). Therefore, to engage in spiritual warfare in blindness is offering yourself for destruction. Discernment of spirits, inspiration of the Spirit and revelation are the ultimate keys to exposing the operations of the kingdom of satan as well as the agents and agencies they use regardless of what dimensions. **You must ask the LORD God to bring you to the place of deeper spirituality. You must be able to infiltrate and penetrate the enemy's territories or domains without exposing your presence or create any suspicion and arouse notice. You must be able to eavesdrop on their agendas and counter their efforts to secretly impact your life.** Careful authority and power always have exceptional intelligence capability. They are always parts of the elements of surprises!

THE ENEMY SAW THE CHARIOTS OF FIRE - 2 Kings 6:17: *Then Elisha prayed, Lord, I pray You, open his eyes that he may see. And the Lord opened the young man's eyes, and he saw, and behold, the mountain was full of horses and chariots of fire round about Elisha.*

Chariots of fire are parts of the formation of heavily armed war vehicles. Similar to armored tanks but they are terrestrial! Their assignments are to use the element of fire to destroy anything like the case of Sodom and Gomorrah. These fire-throwers set ablaze everything on their paths of destruction to reduce it to nothing by fire. The chariots show military posture and as experts in the use of element of fire to exterminate their opponents, there is no way to stop, outrun or escape them. No enemy wants to contend with them because they are destroyers. When God releases chariots of fire, they are set **for catastrophic warfare and a quick devastating job. Here is what you must always remember about the weapons of the glory**: They are equipped beyond measures because God does not give the Spirit by measure, so you are dealing with excessive force because of the full impact. When the LORD God allows these dangerous armies and weapons to suddenly surface, it's to overthrow a nation or kingdom and people regardless of their abilities to fight and no matter what fortification they may have surrounded themselves with. The reason these weapons sometimes appear in warfare is to change the face of the battle to establish the rulership order of the LORD God. You cannot fight Almighty as you cannot All-powerful; therefore, you must retreat or surrender. In the glory, you must relinquish all authority and power or face all authority and power! Anything that exalt itself in the glory is abased whether it is an image, a person, a spirit, a weapon, a nation or kingdom and people! **Call for the chariots of fire and horses of fire like Elijah and release the fire-throwers to demolish or pulverize the enemy's territory or domain and erase it from history! Scotch out their landmarks and landscapes and turn them to desolation!**

BLINDNESS FELL UPON THE ENEMY - 2 Kings 6:18, 20: *And when the Syrians came down to him, Elisha prayed to the Lord, Smite this people with blindness, I pray You. And God smote them with blindness, as Elisha asked. And when they had come into Samaria, Elisha said, Lord open the eyes of these men that they may see. And the Lord opened their* *eyes, and they saw. Behold, they were in the midst of Samaria!*

Acts 13:11: *And now, behold, the hand of the Lord is upon you, and you will be blind, [so blind that you will be] unable to see the sun for a time. Instantly there fell upon him a mist and a darkness, and he groped about seeking persons who would lead him by the hand.*

The human life is full of windows and doors and likewise, the spirit beings and the spirit realms. This is why there are spiritual and physical defenses to secure and protect these windows, doors and gates from intrusion, breaches or unauthorized access. The spirit, soul and body can be attacked and there are spiritual attacks that can impact spirits and humans. Anything that is created can be destroyed so your prayers must be targeted to affect individuals, entities, organizations, regions, offices, positions, nations or kingdoms, etc. Blinding the eyes, deafening the ears or affecting other parts of the body including the heart and the soul are all parts of extreme warfare that the enemy engage to destroy people's lives. When you pray, you must target all aspect of the enemy's aggression including their structures and weapons. You must devastate their lives in many ways to incapacitate their ability to respond. Your weapons are designed to strike different areas of their lives besides taking out their bases and their weapons. **Blind their eyes, command their ears not to hear, paralyze them and speak death upon them. Turn their days into night and reverse the order of the creation like when the LORD God confused the languages of the people. Release strange weapons of the LORD to find them like heat-seeking missiles to obliterate their hiding places. Bankrupt their kingdoms by**

inflicting heavy cost upon them. Ask the LORD of Hosts and Captain of the Hosts to help you. Anything that is created can be dismantled or disabled to render it inoperable or dysfunctional. These are the things that the enemy carry out on the people in the spirit realms daily. Evil has no bounds because it's a nature that creates revolving appetites!

SUNLIGHT INCREASED - 2 Kings 20:11: *So Isaiah the prophet cried to the Lord, and He brought the shadow the ten steps backward by which it had gone down on the sundial of Ahaz.*

The longevity, duration, strength, number, weight or volume of everything can be increased, expanded and reduced. The laws of extraction and retraction can apply. Anything that is controlled by spiritual laws can defy all-natural laws or invalidate the physical functionality. Control goes beyond remote access to engage whole custody and possession. It means to seize the power of control or ability to control as part of ruling with absolute judgment. The sun will not smite you by day and neither the moon by night. We also see the star fighting battle – so everything created in the glory is weaponized to accelerate beyond their normal lives, abilities and operations. When the LORD use elements to do battle, there is no way to stop them. We as the people of God must come to the deeper place to touch the dimensions of the majestic glory of God. Season, time, days, weeks, months, years and ages can be weaponized by adding or taking away. Subtraction and addition as well as increase and multiplication are laws that create either surplus or depletion. The armies of the created works are strike forces but never forget to forge an alliance with the LORD of Hosts and Captain of the Hosts. **To engage the elements, you must hear from the LORD God like Moses, Joshua, Elijah and Elisha. The phenomena of the wonders of the created works are activated by the rulership authority and power of the LORD God!** Let us make man in our image after our likeness and let them have dominion – accessibility to supreme rulership authority and power in God over elements of the created works of God. In the spirit realms, there is regulation and deregulation. There are military, diplomatic, legislative and judicial approaches to dealing with issues or resolute conflicts.

DESTROY THE ENEMY'S FORTIFICATION - Joshua 6:20: *So the people shouted, and the trumpets were blown. When the people heard the sound of the trumpet, they raised a great shout, and [Jericho's] wall fell down in its place, so that the [Israelites] went up into the city, every man straight before him, and they took the city.*

Whatever fortification or security defenses that the enemy has put in place to make your breakthrough harder, you must quickly destroy them. Taking away your enemy's defense is also disorienting their offense. The distraction and confusion are too great because they have to juggle between offense and defense. This is an urgent case of life and death. There is no time for them to evacuate their belongs or rebuild the breached security so they will become desperate – fighting to stay alive or save their lives. Security is part of offense; therefore, you want to deplete and suppress the enemy's ability to resist. You will see that Joshua did not attack the people of

Jericho first but the hardened fortification of the City walls. By plundering the walls of defense, they lost their offenses and Joshua took the City. This is why dimensional warfare prayer targets all enemy infrastructures to dismantle their bases. The asymmetric approach to dimensional warfare makes the battlefield and battlefront harder to defend because every inch of the enemy territory or domain is exposed momentarily. There is always one area or another that the enemy wants to defend more than any other areas but opening all fronts destroys the enemy's courage to continue to stand and fight. The LORD is a man of war and a Master strategist when it comes to epic warfare. **Target every part or area of the enemy's kingdom in your warfare prayer and call for earthquake, thunder, lightning, flood, storm, wind, fire, angels and much more. Ask the LORD God what weapons to engage to destroy the enemy strongholds and plunder his gates and City.**

DON'T ALLOW THE ENEMY TO TAKE A BREAK - Joshua 10:13: *And the sun stood still, and the moon stayed, until the nation took vengeance upon their enemies.*

Sometimes, we hear the scriptures and they sound very basic: We don't see the deeper side or meaning of what they really stand for. The Bible said, *when men sleep, the enemy...* and *He that keepeth Israel neither sleep nor slumber.* It is important to pray for the LORD to open your eyes spiritually so that even when you are asleep, your spiritual eyes are wide open. You can sleep physically with the eyelids closed and suddenly wake up. This is how you know what is happening in your environment or around you. In the spirit realms, slumber is covering your eyelid and even though your eyes are open, the eyelid is closed so you stumble around and fall. You cannot fight the enemy spiritually with your spiritual eyes closed – you want to see everything they are doing and hear what they are saying. You want to know where they are and how many they are. You want to know where they are coming from. It is why in the spirit realms the LORD opens your eyes and ears to see and hear instead of sensing and feeling your way through. Blindness is not an oversight but a real disability! The enemy works when you are not – or you can simply use the term, working over-time! They subject their victims to overlabor as ways to overwhelm their abilities or capacity to continue to respond and systematically destroy their lives. They short-circuit their lives by taking away their rest to subdue and rule! It is the reason the glory gives you rest because of the fullness of the LORD God. Devils like to bombard your life with relentless onslaught even when you are asleep to make it harder for you to defend yourself from their attacks. Anything that is designed to work in season and time cannot function both in season and out of season or over time. It will begin to breakdown quicker so overlabor destroys the longevity of people and the same applies to battle fatigues. You cannot allow your enemy to find rest in the heat of battle because they can reorganize or add extra defensive and offensive measures to drag the fight on forever. The quicker you win is the better for you in realizing the harvest of your hard-fought breakthrough. Joshua could not allow the night to become a deciding factor in dealing with his dangerous enemy and the LORD God ordered him to command the sun to stand still. (See Joshua 10: 10-14). There is suspension in the spirit realms, which applies to all life in the glory. Life is animated and therefore, can be paused like remote control. Be still and know that I am God! When you suffer sleep paralysis, it is to pause your life so you will not function!

YOU ARE GOD'S WEAPON OF WARFARE - Jeremiah 51:20: *You [Cyrus of Persia, soon to conquer Babylon] are My WAR CLUB or maul and weapon of war - for with you I break nations in pieces, with you I destroy kingdoms.*

Everything in the glory is a defense: This is to say that they are not only created to defend against God's purpose or kingdom interest, but they are also equipped to defend themselves against any attack. Everything understands the concept of warfare to some degree and they can all learn the art of war. You hear about self-defense all the time and everywhere and people bearing personal arms or nations or kingdoms stockpiling weapons of war. Territories and domains including other interests are defended as well as personal security and defense. Therefore, we are not exempt from bearing arms or being turned into instruments of war. The anointing for example is used to enhance instrument of war because the Holy Spirit is the Spirit of Might. The Bible said, be **strong** in the LORD and the **power of His might** or mighty power of God. It is not by **might nor by power** but **by my Spirit**. Ye shall receive **power after that the Holy Spirit** has come upon you. I can go on and on! Power is not only to defend but also to attack the enemy. *He teacheth my hands to war, and my fingers to fight. He teacheth my hands to war, so that a bow of steel is broken by my arms.* These Scriptures are incredible because they clearly showed the mighty power of God coming upon individuals and turning them into war machines. You are an instrument of war and it is why the enemy know to attack you before you attack them or destroy their kingdom interest. **Ask the LORD God to anoint you with the Spirit of Might like Samson, David and many others who fought extreme battles and violently destroyed the enemy.** And don't forget you can even go farther into the glory realms where dimensional warfare is beyond what any human can fathom. This is the fullness of the LORD God!

TORRENTS OF RAIN, GREAT HAILSTONES, FIRE AND BRIMSTONE ALL USED FOR WARFARE - Ezekiel 28:23: *For I will send pestilence into her and blood into her streets, and the wounded shall be judged and fall by the sword in the midst of her on every side, and they shall know (understand and realize) that I am the Lord [the Sovereign Ruler, Who calls forth loyalty and obedient service].*

The above Scripture highlights or show a catalogue of powerful weapons of war that are accessible to the people of God in dimensional warfare. Dominion takes great access because you are penetrating and infiltrating different realms, so you need access to various weapons momentarily without having to stop – come out of the realm and then enter back. Unlocking the treasures of Heaven supplies is the only option in dealing with dimensional warfare. The anointing presents you with limited capacity; therefore, you can only achieve levels of success based upon what you have. This means that you must exercise diligent caution to maintain accurate inventory of the level of the outpouring of the Holy Spirit and measure of the power of God in your life. Nature is not controlled by humans, so in epic spiritual warfare you need

Heavens' intervention. The Heavens declare the glory. You need the activation of elemental supports and assistance, which is why the LORD God announces you to the created works as a way to establish a divine network between you and the created works. *"Let us make man in our image after our likeness"* and *"this is my beloved son in whom I am well pleased"* are spiritual introductions and announcements to the created works. It is an important key to establishing eternal order by engaging the alliances and cooperation – the collaboration and corroboration of elements to assist in fulfilling the purpose of God for your life. "All things must work together" from spiritual perspective – or according to the purpose of God and your destiny. Passage to your destination is critical to fulfilling God's purpose for your life. Besides angels helping you, elements are parts of your backup supports and you can see how many battles they have helped different men of God to win throughout the Bible. The Bible said, as it is Heaven so also in the Earth! This is to show that Heaven uses the elements to do extreme battles for the glory of the LORD God. You can ruin your enemy's seasons and confuse their times by changing the physical laws with the spiritual laws! **It is the reason you do not carry weapons around in the glory because you are announced and suddenly introduced to concealed or hidden armies of God to help you in dimensional warfare. These armies or weapons appear momentarily to give you unprecedented power to triumph over your enemy.** It is how you subdue and rule or operate in dominion!

DISARM YOUR ENEMY - Ezekiel 39:3: *And I will smite your bow from your left hand and will cause your arrows to* *fall out of your right hand.*

Warfare is all about targeting different components of the enemies' setup: structures, weapons, locations, personnel and logistics – anything and everything that will give the enemy advantage over you. You must look at the air, the land, the water, the elements, the people and the animals – spiritually and physically. You must leave no stone unturned! Disarming your enemy takes great work depending on how widely prepared or how many bases of operation they have established. You must understand that they are going to deploy their assets from multiple locations and positions involving different ranks and weapons. Besides arming individual soldiers, the nation or kingdom has weapons' depot – manufacturing plants or factories and weapons storages scattered everywhere for strategic purposes. When you are under attack, you must target the enemy including their weapons: depots, storages, manufacturing plants or factories, etc. The weapons are what they will use to hurt you so you must know to quickly disarm them. The quicker you achieve the goal is the easier it becomes to win the battle. Sometimes, you must cut off their backup supports from coming to assist in resisting your effort to win. Equipment can malfunction and weapons can be destroyed. **In your prayer warfare, command their weapons to malfunction and release counter weapons to destroy them and force the enemy soldiers to surrender!** They cannot fight with nothing! Most importantly, they will not fully respect your authority and power if you leave them with the ability and capability to continue to fight you back.

BRING DEATH UPON YOUR ENEMY - Ezekiel 39:4-5:

You shall fall [dead] upon the mountains of Israel, you and all your hosts and the peoples who are with you. I will give you to the ravenous birds of every sort and to the beasts of the field to be devoured. You shall fall in the open field, for I have spoken [it],' says the Lord God.

Acts 5:5, 10: *Upon hearing these words, Ananias fell down and died. And great dread and terror took possession of all who heard of it. And instantly she fell down at his feet and died; and the young men entering found her dead, and they carried her out and buried her beside her husband.*

If life is given, life can also be taken away! Speaking death is part of decree and declaration to condemn according to the Word of the LORD. God can authorize death and his people can speak death. Life and death are in the power of the tongue or utterance. Death utterance is equivalent to death sentence, which is stripping away a person's life to end it or terminate the existence. The execution of the order of death is like carrying out Heaven's order of judgment. Releasing weapons of death is to literally kill and destroy so it's not a symbolic term or figment of imagination. There is power to give life and power to kill or take away life. Your enemies can fall dead by the thousands and tens of thousands or even innumerable. Casualties can multiple upon the enemy – sowing chaos in their midst or reduce their numbers and paralyze their abilities to remain fighting. An angel of the LORD killed 185, 000 Assyrian soldiers overnight, which is a mass slaughter. Calling death upon your enemy is inflicting great pain upon the kingdom they represent and reducing the kingdom ability by wiping out a great number of the loyal fighters! When nations or kingdoms begin to take great losses including weapons, they will not hesitate to abandon the fight or surrender. Weapons of death can cause tremendous casualties and likewise, the words of the people of God under the legitimate authority and power of God can wreak havoc on the enemy. The Earth is the LORD's and the fullness thereof, so everything belongs to God and accessible to the people of God including the authority and power to banish from the Earth and destroy evil works against humanity. **The Son of God was manifested that He might destroy the works the devils, and the wicked are sons of the devils, who are undertaking his assignments to do evil!**

STOP THE POWER OF THE ENEMY - Daniel 3:25: *He answered, Behold, I see four men loose, walking in the midst of the fire, and they are not hurt! And the form of the fourth is like a son of the gods!*

Taking away power from the enemy is embarrassing him and his kingdom. It is openly degrading his authority and power, and demoralizing his loyal agents. It is uncovering his deception and lies and establishing the truth. When the enemy threatens to destroy your life and the power of God descends and destroys his power, your God will be revered by all. People will turn away from the enemy to honor the name of the LORD like the case of the three Hebrew boys in the furnace of fire. The LORD God took away power from the enemy's fire and they were not burned. The king issued a decree – honoring the God that these three boys serve. The establishment of the kingdom of Heaven takes radical approach because *the Kingdom of Heaven suffereth violent and the violent taketh it by force.* Violent force is part of resistant power, which is beyond statements of confessions. You are risking it all to gain extraordinary response. It is going where no one has been and daring the impossible so you are trespassing into the domain that only the LORD God whom all things are possible may rescue you. Elements, objects and subjects that produce death are real threats; therefore, they are not combated by religious citations or ceremonial eulogies. **You are coming eye-to-eye with the sting of death. You need extinguishing power of God! You need degrading and destabilizing power of God! You need tranquilizer to incapacitate your enemy. You need high voltage power of God! You need atomic energy! You need electromagnetic power of God to reduce everything and short-circuit the operations of the enemy.** You must pray for the unusual power of God and extraordinary weapons of warfare.

SILENCE THE ENEMY AND DESTROY THEIR WORKS

- Daniel 6:22: My God has sent His angel and has shut the lions' mouths so that they have not hurt me, because I was found innocent and blameless before Him; and also before you, O king, [as you very well know] I have done no harm or wrong.

When the mouth of the enemy is risen up against you in judgment – when the enemy issue a decree or ruling against your life and released his agents and agencies to execute the orders, you must silence or stop them from enforcing the orders. You can invoke the authority and power of God to over-rule the enemy's judgment against your life. Whether their means of enforcement is spiritual or physical, you can stop the agents or agencies from following the orders. The Bible said, resist the devil

– you must resist his order of arrest and refuse the execution of his kingdom authority and power against you. Part of the enemy fulfilling the order of judgment is acting or behaving in the manner, which the decree outlined. There is no weapon formed against you that shall prosper, and any tongue risen against you in judgment, thou shall condemn. You must rise to the occasion and sabotage their operations or the weapons will function against you and the judgment of the enemy will be executed upon you. There is a place of stronger authority and power in God that elements only obey the voice of the LORD God and the enemy cannot use the created works of God to fight against the purpose of God for your life. When the water rose up against Jesus and the disciples, He silenced the storm and calmed it. You must deprive the enemy the rights to use God's created works to do evil and wickedness. This is tightening the noose around the neck of his kingdom to diminish the expansion and cutting off the extension. By limiting the geographical reach and impacting the demographic, you curtail the rise of his kingdom by depleting the assets and resources. Nations or Kingdom and people can go bankrupt – spiritually and physically because as it is in Heaven so also in the Earth. The secret is engaging the authority and power of the kingdom of Heaven! **When you pray say, thine Kingdom come, thy will (your purpose) be done in the Earth as it is in Heaven. Declare the rulership decree of the LORD God to get every created work of God to refrain from taking orders from the kingdom of satan and the agents or agencies. Turn the created works of God against them so they will not harbor or give them hiding places to operate against the purpose of God. Command the Heavens to declare the glory of God. And remember that the Earth is the**

LORD's and the fullness thereof!

SEND GOD'S ELEMENTS TO SWALLOW THE ENEMY
- Jonah 1:17: *Now the Lord had prepared and appointed a great fish to swallow up Jonah. And Jonah was in the belly of the fish three days and three nights. Jonah 2:10 And the Lord spoke to the fish, and it vomited out Jonah upon the dry land.*

Some people of God may not understand the supernatural implication of consuming an opponent to retain and detain the culprit. However, it's the very characteristic behavior of the glory to consume – by overshadowing to eclipse or hide or take into custody. Binding and losing are not limited to keeping the enemy in chains or declaration of restraining order but consuming the enemy. The history of the enemy is not only erased from the record of life, the trace of the opponent's life is diminished. When the ground open to swallow or when the snake of Moses swallowed the snakes of Pharaoh's magicians, there was no way to connect with their whereabouts. It also includes when people are translated into the glory like Enoch, the body of Moses, the body of Elijah and Jesus Christ, none of their bodies could be found. Arrest warrants are issued by the decrees of the LORD God because ruling supreme turns every word of the LORD God into a decree and the elements can respond intelligently because of the power revelation. They know who they are commanded to look for or where to attack. Likewise, anything that is swallowed by the enemy can be vomited out or returned back. The glory is a defense so its undertaking spiritual and physical measures to fulfill the order of Heaven in the Earth and everywhere else. It is also the way to disarm contentious enemies to deprive them of raising up counter-actions or resisting. The death and burial of the armies of Egypt and their weapons of war in the red sea was a classic example of the revelation of the glory because the glory releases the judgment of the LORD God to consume the enemy. Always, the enemy cannot run, hide or escape! **As you begin to advance towards the threshold of dimensional warfare, the realms of God will suddenly open to allow you to adopt the spiritual order of life and functionality. You become like Him and function like Him because your whole life is consumed by Him. Consuming your enemies is burying them or making them disappear so they will be no more**! This is part of the revelation of the beginning and end or the termination and extinction of anything that is created by God. Rulership always deals with sovereignty!

DESTROY THE HABITATION OF THE WICKED - Haggai 1:9: *You looked for much [harvest], and behold it came to little; and even when you brought that home, I blew it away. Why?' says the Lord of hosts. 'Because of My house, which lies waste while you yourselves run each man to his own house [eager to build and adorn it].*

You can attack and dismantle the enemy's infrastructures or bases of operations – leaving them with no place to retreat or replenish. Stranded enemy is exposed to great danger. Shelter is part of defense so destroying their bases is taking away their lifelines. When the LORD deal with his enemy, they will experience harsh realities. Because many people of God don't come to the place of realities with God, they lack devasting punch of God's great power against their enemies. They give the enemy leverage to continue to advance against them instead of stopping them on their tracks or causing great panic to fall upon them. The LORD God does not fight to leave the enemy standing so the people of God must know to keep asking the LORD for catastrophic weapons against the enemy to annihilate them. History is not kind to the opposers of God and trespassers against His commandments. Therefore, the people of God always have an advantage against the enemy regardless of how many or how powerful they may be. **Never leave the enemy with options! You must terrorize the enemy with the atomic power of God over your life so they will bow down to the LORD God that you worship and serve!** Warfare is not all about being nice or showing courtesy, which is why there are treaties and formal agreements to end wars. Warfare is win or lose!

ENGAGE THE POWER OF SPIRITUAL SUPPLIES:

FOOD MULTIPLIED - Matthew 14:20: *And they all ate and were satisfied. And they picked up twelve [small hand] baskets full of the broken pieces left over. And those who ate were about 5,000 men, not including women and children.*

Matthew 15:36: *He took the seven loaves and the fish, and when He had given thanks, He broke them and gave them to the disciples, and the disciples gave them to the people. Those who ate were 4,000 men, not including the women and the children.*

In every warfare, there is the humanitarian aspect or you will violate the spiritual and natural orders of life. There are those who deserve mercy and grace so when the glory shows up, the LORD God is merciful and gracious to whom He will. Remember that his glory reveals his judgment! The temptation is too great when you begin to experience extraordinary authority and power. **You must not do evil or target the innocent. You must not take falsely from others or violet the guiding principles of the commandments of the LORD or abuse the grace of God. You must not serve the interest of the enemy for self-gain or compromise the order of God.** Servitude and obedience are the bedrock of humility so pride will not take root in your life. To do good is better than to do evil. Righteousness and holiness are parts of the nature of God and His Kingdom is established upon His nature, and not just only by His power. *His power is the key to enforcement but His life is the secret to His establishment.* He rains upon the righteous and the wicked to demonstrate equality without prejudice, and yet the LORD God has preference to exalt and to bring down. I was hungry and you fed me. I was naked and you clothed me. I was in prison and you visited me. Always, the needs of the general public are in His agenda even when they are not yet saved and washed by the blood of the Lamb. This is humanitarian, which is separate from eternal judgment! Do good works to others and don't judge them critically in their points of needs and desperations, but help lift them up through prayers and personal generosity. *And as ye go, preach, saying, The kingdom of heaven is at hand. Heal the sick, cleanse the lepers, raise the dead, cast out devils: freely ye have received, freely give* (Matthew 10:7-8).

WALKING ON WATER - Matthew 14:26, 29: *And when the disciples saw Him walking on the sea, they were terrified and said, 'It is a ghost!' And they screamed out with fright. He said, Come! So Peter got out of the boat and walked on the water, and he came toward JESUS.*

The temperature and heartbeat of faith is not the same with operating in the age of innocence. Without knowing fear, you cannot operate under the power of fear. Without knowing death, you cannot operate under the fear of death. The age of innocence is free from the knowledge of evil and the fear of harm, failure and death. From spiritual perspective, we can begin to understand what is written in the Word of God. When you pass through the water, you shall not drown and when you pass through the fire, it shall not burn you. Shifting from the natural to the spirit creates a different law that defies the natural-laws. Wonders are parts of the exhibitions of unusual spiritual capacities. Eye hath not seen, ear hath not heard, and neither hath entered the heart of man. The human faculties are elementary to spiritual fullness and often no amount of human perception, concept, ideology, theory, belief and faith can fathom the depth of spiritual mysteries. Walking on the water is beyond academic formula because it's a spiritual phenomenon. This is not just only faith but coming in contact with extraordinary power! The impossible is only achieved through the power that makes all things possible. **You must come to the place where the enemy's weapons no longer have any effect against you and where the fear of the enemy is no longer a concern for you. Ask the LORD to reveal his fear on your life and to establish his great fear over your enemy. They will tremble at your voice and shiver before your presence.**

ENGAGE THE POWER OF SPIRITUAL SUPPLIES:

FISH GAVE OUT MONEY - Matthew 17:27: *However, in*

order not to give offense and cause them to stumble [that is, to cause them to judge unfavorably and unjustly] go down to the sea and throw in a hook. Take the first fish that comes up, and when you open its mouth you will find there a shekel. Take it and give it to them to pay the temple tax for Me and for yourself.

Spiritual supplies are not limited to the human resources, but the vast created works of God whether spiritually and physically. The challenge is that many people of God have not come to the place of spiritual unification to realize the heavenly materialization in the physical. Many resources are hidden under the ground and so many resources are above and likewise, in the waters, etc. Extracting these resources will more than suffice the needs of the human race for many generations. If a fish would release money to pay for tax bills, we can only imagine where else our spiritual supplies are hidden until we access them. This is where we need spiritual guidance: We need inspiration of the Spirit and revelation of God to access our hidden inheritance. The earth is the LORD's and the fullness thereof. Often, we think that our blessings will only come through one source, which is thinking logically rather than spiritually. We are in a generation that lack spirituality because the modern society focus on academic achievements more than spiritual advancement. Ravens brought meat and bread to Elijah! **There are no bounds to the overwhelming spiritual wonders of the works of God so we must see beyond our abilities to reason logically. Logic is short-sightedness because the spirit realms are hidden and we must believe God, exercise faith in Him until we know His faithfulness.** With God nothing shall be impossible!

WONDER OF THE BIRTH OF JESUS - Luke 1:35: *Then the angel said to her, The Holy Spirit will come upon you, and **the power of the Most High will overshadow you** [like a shining cloud]; and so the holy (pure, sinless) thing (offspring) which shall be born of you will be called the Son of God.*

If you are not familiar with a body-armor; the overshadowing of the glory is like wearing a body-armor because you are encased or incubated in God. The Bible said, *the glory is a defense.* The glory defense is activation of divine intervention in degree that it is impossible to avert the purpose of God. (See Isaiah 4:5; 14:24; Zechariah 2:5; Luke 1:37). There is a difference between fighting alongside an armor-bearer and moving in the realms of God. When the glory overshadows, no enemy can breach the perimeter or they will be stricken dead. And I am talking about spiritually and physically. It is why people receive immediate deliverance and freedom in the atmosphere of the glory. It is also the reason everything can live eternally without destruction from any power. The impossible belong in the atmosphere of the glory because of the revelation of the person of God beyond the manifested presence of his Holy Spirit. Without access to the realms of God, you cannot go in there! Everything in the glory are used to create redundancy like air defenses of nations or kingdoms. You trespass at your own judgment because whatever decision that is taken to deal with you is what you deserve. The coming of Jesus Christ was so important that the LORD God applied overwhelming security measures to protect the child in the womb. Mary was overshadowed by the glory (Luke 1:35). We see how the enemy pursued after his life when IIe was born but God deployed angels to warn the parents to escape the land. Overshadowing of the glory is the final screw against the enemy seeking to abort the original plan of God. Original plans of God are sensitive matters that deserve all the attention because they are parts of the orders of restitution and restoration of all things. **Always pray to experience the glory of God in your life. And ask the LORD God to help you pay the great price of moving in the glory realms.** *Then Satan answered the LORD, and said, Doth Job fear God for nought? Hast not thou made an hedge about him, and about his house, and about all that he hath on every side?* (Job 1:9-10a).

ANGEL USED TO RELEASE PRISONER - Acts 5:18, 19: *They seized and arrested the apostles (special messengers) and put them in the public jail. But during the night an angel of the Lord opened the prison doors and, leading them out....*

In every war, there are injuries, wounds and death but we must not forget about prisoners of war – those captured alive and taken into the enemy's custodies. We have to see that a hero is not always a winner because bravery and courage are part of great achievements. Nations or kingdoms negotiate to exchange their prisoners of war and people wonder why they are honored as heroes when they were captured in battles. They see a hero as always, a winner and not a loser! I want you to understand that the ability to release imprisoned war hero is part of winning a battle! The reason is that the more soldiers that return alive from the battlefield and the battlefront are more reasons to count the war as great success. Besides rescue operations, nations or kingdoms can negotiate diplomatically to save the lives of their missing soldiers. The kingdom of Heaven also uses diplomatic and rescue efforts to liberate the people of God whose lives are in danger. Defending against their lives is one thing and moving to save their lives is another. Sometimes, purpose is prioritized over sacrificing a life and sometimes, lives are prioritized over a purpose, so we have to see the difference between a kingdom and personal life! Angels are encamped round about the people of God – depending on the severity of their work assignments and some people of God have Guardian angels. Warrior Angels are deployed for war and Guardian Angels are assigned to personal protection and security besides, assisting them to fulfil certain goals. In either case, they work to help the people of God win. **Always, ask the LORD God to deploy his angels around you to help you with spiritual warfare and other important work assignments. They can save your life even in most dangerous situations!**

POWER OF REVELATION – TO DISAPPEAR OR APPEAR - Acts 8:38, 39, 40: *And he ordered that the chariot be stopped; and both Philip and the eunuch went down into the water, and [Philip] baptized him. And when they came up out of the water, the Spirit of the Lord [suddenly] caught away Philip; and the eunuch saw him no more, and he went on his way rejoicing. But Philip was found at Azotus...*

If you are not familiar with how the glory of God works, you will be left without the sudden movement of the LORD God. The great move of God is not the same with how the manifested presence of his Holy Spirit operates through people. God is a Spirit (John 4:24). The deeper realms of the spirit create a void and a vacuum without the power of revelation to peer into the depth or dimension. You will be waiting and waiting without knowing that everything is already over. Another important factor is that frustration and desperation can lead to despair in your life. Without knowing his whereabout and what He is doing, you can go into a panic mode, and it's not a matter of believing God or having faith in God. Both the gift of faith and measures of faith cannot sustain your life through the eternal realm. You need faithfulness, which is the character or life of God. Without entering his life, you will lose everything in this dimension of God. Some people even with the anointing have turned their weapons on themselves in the heat of battles because of great desperation. Not knowing where to turn, escape or hide from the enemy, they fell on their own sword or asked the armor-bearer to slay them by the sword. You see Elijah asking the LORD God to take away his life when Jezebel pressed the panic button of his life by threatening to cut his head off. The power of revelation can hide you from the enemy even in the broad day light: Now, they see you and then, they see you not. Now, they hear you and then, they hear you not. Suddenly, disappearing and appearing again will make your enemy realize that things are not normal. They will recognize that they are dealing with a different species that are not subjected to the natural laws. It is engaging the fullness of the life and power of the Spirit and using both the spirit and physical realms to transit momentarily. Spirits can easily hide from the humans even when they are before their presence unless their eyes are opened to see or they are translated to enter the spirit realms. The same applies to neutralizing the enemy's death blow and destroying the power of death by the power of creation and the power of resurrection. There is whole transformation that alters your form and appearance besides stopping the power of death! And there is power to ascend and descend or defy gravity, depth, width, length and height! **Pray for the power of revelation to see and hear in the spirit realms and to pierce the spirit realms. Always, the power of revelation works together with the power of creation, the power of resurrection and the power of ascension to fully enter the spirit realms in a moment!**

EARTHQUAKE USED TO RELEASE PRISONERS - Acts 16:26: *Suddenly there was a great earthquake, so that the very foundations of the prison were shaken; and at once all the doors were opened and everyone's shackles were unfastened.*

Acts 12:7, 10: *And suddenly an angel of the Lord appeared [standing beside him], and a light shone in the place where he was. And the angel gently smote Peter on the side and awakened him, saying, Get up quickly! And the chains fell off his hands. When they had passed through the first guard and the second, they came to the iron gate which leads into the city. Of its own accord [the gate] swung open, and they went out and passed on through one street; and at once the angel left him.*

Tearing through the enemy's fortification or infiltrating and penetrating their defenses are all part of subduing and ruling. It's a demonstration of superior or unstoppable power! Whether the operation involves high-tech, special operation forces, angels, humans, elements and whatever other means, it is reversing victory and conquer. It is like taking away the keys of death and hell! The spoils of war are not only the golden trophies or loads of artifacts and the plundering of the mineral resources. The captured soldiers are also greater parts of the spoils of war. Sometimes, they are bargaining chips when it comes to negotiating a cease fire. Rescuing them are slaps on the face. Its undermining the ability of the enemy to safeguard important achievement and accomplishment. With Elijah the prophet of glory, the ravens brought him bread and flesh to sustain his life instead of waiting for him to fall dead. Always, God will turn evil for good! If the enemy take you hostage or impose a retaining order against your life, you must release the earthquake of God great power that works like the natural earthquake. The earthquake power of God is like a bunker-bursting missile! When Heaven respond to deliver trapped people of God from the enemy's prisons, it is demonstrating the great power of God to save, deliver and rescue from the uttermost! The operation sets the camp of the people of God ablaze with the fire of courage and defiant faith to stand and resist the enemy at all cost. It is mocking the enemy by reversing the kingdom gain. Kingdoms love popularity and the news of how dreadful their warriors and weapons of war are. They trumpet and publicize their accomplishments everywhere to strike terror in the hearts of opposing nations or kingdoms. One thing so profound about the great power of the LORD God is that both elements, angels and humans can do the impossible by engaging the fullness of God. The Bible said, *for with God nothing shall be impossible* (Luke 1:37).

VERNOMOUS SNAKE BITE HAD NO POWER - Acts 28:3, 5: *Now Paul had gathered a bundle of sticks, and he was laying them on the fire when a viper crawled out because of the heat and fastened itself on his hand. Then [Paul simply] shook off the small creature into the fire and suffered no evil effects.*

Neutralizing the powers of the enemy is defending

against the abilities to affect you in the case of sudden impacts. Concealed weapons are living nightmares because they are unsuspecting. This is to say that their impacts are death-blows! The surprise attacks of the enemy are to take out their opponents without suspicion so the operations are precise. Decoys and proxies are setup to achieve close proximity and inflict damaging wounds, injuries or death. The antidote of the great power of God is the only thing that can rescue an individual that find him or herself in such predicament. The enemy is subtle and deceptive! Genesis Chapter 3 can give you a deeper understanding of how the enemy can ambush and prey on their victims even when they are highly prepared. The Bible said, *no weapons formed against thee shall prosper...* and *Behold, I give unto you power to tread on serpents and scorpions, and over all the power of the enemy: and nothing shall by any means hurt you* (Isaiah 54:17; 55: Luke 10:19). You must know that your life has to be greatly overwhelmed by the power of God to diffuse and neutralize the enemy's power to destroy your life. The degree to which your life is empowered will determine your safety – at all times!

The sixth commandment of God in the Bible is, "*THOU SHALL NOT COMMIT MURDER*! The King James Version says "*Thou shall not kill*", nevertheless, when you are defending yourself, you are not committing murder or killing.

Finally, you must never forget to show mercy, kindness and love to those who recognize their evil ways and repent sincerely unto the LORD. Be patient and always quick to forgive others, and remember that their repentance is crying out to the LORD because of the consequences of their actions or behaviors. It is like raising up a white flag in the heat of battle to surrender from continuing to resist. It is saying that you have had enough and you can no longer remain in the battle. A true repentance will produce a change of heart -- ask the LORD to help you in your decision-making, you don't want to accept a trojan horse or open yourself to a decoy and become victimized in a proxy warfare. Judge all things and inquire concerning all things! Never kill a surrendering enemy because they are parts of the innocent blood and the cries of their blood will turn the battle against you. This is why the message of the gospel is offered or presented to all, and why you must heal those who need healing, deliver those who need deliverance. Clothe those who need shelter, visit those who are in prison. Do good to those who do you evil but don't forget to report their evils to the LORD. Every warfare has good in it, and you must never mix the good with evil or taint the good with evil. This is the balance of righteousness and justice!

Author's Note of Thanks

My beloved family Pastor Minnie and Walter Archy, New Castle, Delaware. Brother and a great servant of God, Bishop Philips and Debra Banini, Host of Jubilee Radio, Glory Cathedral, GA. Archbishop Angelo M. Rosario and Bishop Nancy Rosario, Bronx Clergy Task Force, Bronx, NY. Dr. Wayne Millington, Raising of the Dead Ministries, Brooklyn, NY. Helene Oord, International Liaison/ PR, Embassy of God, Kiev, Ukraine. Nathan and Phoebe Okoli, World Liberation Ministries, Nigeria and USA. My good friend, Pastor Joseph Lyron, Brooklyn, NY. Apostle Fred Opoku-Gyimah, D.D., D.Th, Pentecostal Redeemer's Temple, Inc. Dear Beloved Sister Dr. Marilyn John, Evangelist/Prophetess, Brooklyn, NY. Wonderful Sister Precious C. Aneji, Esq. My Dear Sister, Sharon Johnson, Brooklyn, NY. Dr. S. Wayne Stokeling, Pastor, St. John Baptist Church, Brooklyn, NY. Pastor Mark A. Hinton. Dear beloved Pastor David Olivencia, East New York Miracle Ministry, Brooklyn, NY. Prophet Joseph Elias, true friend.

Rev. Dennis Dillon, Publisher, New York Christian Times and Senior Pastor, Brooklyn Christian Center, NY. Elder James R. Ray, Pastor of New Covenant Church of Christ, Brooklyn, NY. Bishop Carlton J. Walters, Church of God of Prophecy, Brooklyn, NY. Eddy Onyia, Pastor, Glory of God Ministries, Brooklyn, NY. Bishop Roderick Caesar and Pastor Beverly Caesar, Bethel Gospel

Tabernacle, Jamaica, NY. Bishop R.A. Austin and Min. Esme Austin, Mt. Olive Pentecostal Church of Faith, Brooklyn, NY. Bishop Vernie Russell Jr., D.D., Pastor, Mt. Carmel Baptist Church, Norfolk, VA. Rev. Washington L. and Dorothy Lundy, Evening Star Baptist Church, Brooklyn, NY. Overseer Jacqueline Mendoza, East New York Miracle Ministry, Brooklyn, NY. Elder James Fawundu, Pastor, Shiloh Pentecostal Assembly, Brooklyn, NY. Bishop Jacqueline Brown, International House of Prayer, Brooklyn, NY. Pastor Terry and Evangelist Joyce Lee, Pastors, Byways and Hedges Youth for Christ Ministries, Brooklyn, NY.

Pastor Lorenzo and Maxine Williamson, New Deeper Life Tabernacle Outreach Ministries, Brooklyn, NY. Pastor Orlando and Yvette Findlayter, New Hope Christian Fellowship, Brooklyn, NY. Pastor Femi and Philomena Alabi, Bethel of Praise Ministries, Brooklyn, NY. Dear beloved Sister Sharon Bennett, Gospel Rail Productions, Brooklyn, NY. Apostle Chinedu Adigwe, Alpha Bible Church International, Lagos, Nigeria. And to the millions of wonderful men and women of God all around the world who have stood their ground and obeyed the voice of God. You have been a major source of encouragement. You are important in the Kingdom. May God continue to prosper you and your ministries for the glory of His Dear Son and our Lord and Savior, Jesus Christ.

BIBLIOGRAPHY

Adam, David. *Flame in My Heart.* Harrisburg, PA: Morehouse Group, 1998.

Ahn, Sue, et. al. *The Threshold of Glory.* Shippensburg, PA: Destiny Image Publishers, 2000.

Bevere, John. *Breaking Intimidation.* Orlando, FL: Creation House, 1995.

Bosworth, F.F. *Christ the Healer.* Old Tappan, NJ: Fleming H. Revell, 1973.

Brown, Rebecca. *Becoming a Vessel of Honor.* Woodburn, OR: Fortress Books. 1992.

He Came to Set the Captives Free. New Kensington, PA: Whitaker House, 1997.

Prepare for War. New Kensington, PA: Whitaker House, 1997.

Unbroken Curses. Springdale, PA: Whitaker House, 1995.

Brown, Stephen W. *Follow the Wind.* Grand Rapids, MI: Baker Books, 1999.

Buckingham, Jamie. *Daughter of Destiny: Kathryn Kuhlman, Her Story.* Plainfield, NJ: Logos International, 1976.

Cerullo, Morris. *The Last Great Anointing.* Ventura, CA: Renew, 1999.

Chambers, Oswald. *My Utmost for His Highest.* New York, NY: Dodd, Mead & Company, 1935.

Cymbala, Jim. *Fresh Wind, Fresh Fire.* Grand Rapids, MI: Zondervan, 2003.

Dawson, Joy. *Intercession, Thrilling and Fulfilling.* Seattle, WA: YWAM Publishers, 1997.

Intimate Friendship With God. Old Tappan, NJ: Chosen Books, 1986.

Dollar, Creflo A. *Understanding God's Purpose for the Anointing.* New York, NY: Creflo Dollar Ministries, 1992.

Uprooting the Spirit of Fear. Tulsa, OK: Harrison House, 2002.

Fenelon, Francois. *Fenelon: Meditations on the Heart of God.* Brewster, MA: Paraclete Press, 1997.

Talking With God. Brewster, MA: Paraclete Press, 1997.

The Royal Way of the Cross. Orleans, MA: Paraclete Press, 1982.

Finney, Charles G. *God's Call.* New Kensington, PA: Whitaker House, 1999.

Power From on High. Springdale, PA: Whitaker House, 1996.

The Secret of Faith. New Kensington, PA: Whitaker House, 1999.

Guyon, Madame. *Experiencing God Through Prayer.* Springdale, PA: Whitaker House, 1984.

Union With God. Sargent, GA: The Seed Sowers, 1981.

Hagin, Kenneth E. *Healing Forever Settled.* Tulsa, OK: K. Hagin Ministries, 1989.

Plans, Purposes, & Pursuits. Tulsa, OK: Faith Library Publications, 1988.

The Believer's Authority. Tulsa, OK: Faith Library Publications, 1984.

Hammond, Frank, and Ida Mae Hammond. *Pigs in the Parlor.* Kirkwood, MO: Impact Books, 1973.

Hammond, Frank D. *Our Warfare: Against Demons & Territorial Spirits.* Kirkwood, MO: Impact Books, 1991, 1994.

Demons and Deliverance in the Ministry of Jesus. Kirkwood, MO: Impact Books, 1991.

Herzog, David. *Mysteries of the Glory Unveiled.* Hagerstown, MD: McDougal Pub., 2000.

Hinn, Benny. *Good Morning Holy Spirit.* Nashville, TN: T. Publishers, 1990.

He Touched Me. Nashville, TN: Thomas Nelson, 1999.

The Anointing. Nashville, TN: Thomas Nelson Books, 1992.

The Biblical Road to Blessing. Nashville, TN: Thomas Nelson, Inc, 1997.

This Is Your Day for a Miracle. Lake Mary, FL: Creation House, 1996.

H inn, Sam. *Changed in His Presence.* Orlando, FL: Creation House, 1995.

Jakes, T. D. *Loose That Man and Let Him Go!* Tulsa, OK: Bethany House, 1996.

Naked and Not Ashamed. Shippensburg, PA: Treasure House, 1995.

Why? Because You Are Anointed. Bakersfield, CA: Pneuma Life Pub., 1995.

Joyner, Rick. *The Call.* New Kensington, PA: Whitaker House, 1999.

The Final Quest. New Kensington, PA: Whitaker House, 1996.

The Prophetic Ministry. Charlotte, NC: Morning Star Pub., 1997.

Kuhlman, Kathryn. *Healing Words.* Orlando, FL: Creation House, 1997.

I Believe in Miracles. North Brunswick, NJ: Bridge-Logos Pub., 1990.

Lake, Dr. John G., Gordon Lindsay, ed. *Spiritual Hunger and Other Sermons*. Dallas, TX: Christ for the Nations, 1996.

Liardon, Roberts. *God's Generals*. New Kensington, PA: Whitaker House, 2003.

McCullough, Jacqueline. *Daily Moments With God: In Quietness & Confidence*. Bakersfield, CA: Pneuma Life Publishing, 1996.

Meyer, Joyce. *Battlefield of the Mind*. Tulsa, OK: Harrison House, 1995.

Murray, Andrew. *Divine Healing*. New Kensington, PA: Whitaker House, 1982.

The Spirit of Christ. Minneapolis, MN: Bethany House Publishers, 1984.

Nee, Watchman. *The Spiritual Man*. New York, NY: Christian Fellowship Publishers, 1968.

Parsley, Rod. *No More Crumbs*. Lake Mary, FL: Creation House, 1997.

Reidt, Wilford. *John G. Lake: A Man Without Compromise*. Tulsa, OK: Harrison House, 1981.

Schambach, R.W. *I Shall Not Want,* Tulsa, OK: Harrison House, 1990.

Shattles, Jim. *Revival Fire and Glory*. Hagerstown, MD: McDougal Publishing, 1999.

Spurgeon, Charles. *Spurgeon on Prayer & Spiritual Warfare.* New Kensington, PA: Whitaker House, 1998.

Sumrall, Lester. *Angels to Help You.* New Kensington, PA: Whitaker House, 1999.

Pioneers of Faith. Tulsa, OK: Harrison House, 1995.

Tari, Mel. *Like a Mighty Wind.* Carol Stream, IL: Creation House, 1971.

The Gentle Breeze of Jesus. Carol Stream, IL: Creation House, 1974.

Tenney, Tommy. *The God Chasers.* Shippensburg, PA: Destiny Image Publishers, 1998.

Torrey, R. A. *How to Obtain Fullness of Power.* New Kensington, PA: Whitaker House, 1984.

Unger, Merrill F. *Demons in the World Today.* Wheaton, IL: Tyndale House Publishers, 1971.

Walters, Kathie. *Celtic Flames.* Macon, GA: Good News Ministries, 1999.

Columba: The Celtic Dove. Macon, GA: Good News Ministries, 1999.

Ward Heflin, Ruth. *Glory.* Hagerstown, MD: McDougal Publishing Company, 1990.

Golden Glory. Hagerstown, MD: McDougal Publishing Company, 2000.

Harvest Glory: I Ask for the Nations. Hagerstown, MD: McDougal Publishing Company, 1999.

Unifying Glory. Hagerstown, MD: McDougal Publishing Company, 2000.

Wigglesworth, Smith, and Wayne E. Warner. *The Anointing of His Spirit*. Ann Arbor, MI: Vine Books, 1994.

Ever Increasing Faith. New Kensington, PA: Whitaker House, 2000.

Smith Wigglesworth on Healing. New Kensington, PA: Whitaker House, 1999.

Smith Wigglesworth on Power to Serve. New Kensington, PA: Whitaker House, 1998.

Woodworth-Etter, Maria, and Larry Keefauver. *The Original Maria Woodworth-Etter Devotional*. Orlando, FL: Creation House, 1997.

A Diary of Signs & Wonders. Tulsa, OK: Harrison House, 1980.

The Holy Spirit. New Kensington, PA: Whitaker House, 1998

ABOUT THE AUTHOR

Apostle (Dr.) John King Hill received the call of God six months after he gave his heart to the Lord Jesus in 1986. Although Apostle John King Hill has experienced the power of God and seen the miraculous—tumors vanished; deaf ears made to hear; canes abandoned; cancer cells die; ulcers, arthritis, terminal illnesses, various sicknesses and diseases healed; demons cast out; barren wombs conceived; the power of addictions broken; curses removed; jobs restored; lives transformed; and prayers dramatically answered—his heart has never ceased to cry for more, much more, and greater power of God. In 1997 at a conference by Benny Hinn (a man he now calls his spiritual father and mentor), Apostle John King Hill experienced an unusual encounter with the person of the Holy Spirit that utterly marked his life and ministry. Today, Apostle John King Hill's ministry has taken an explosive turn by the glorious power of God. There have been overwhelmingly unusual displays of God's glorious power in several of Apostle John King Hill's meetings, both nationally and internationally.

The ministry of Apostle John King Hill is defined by the radical demonstration of God's power which denies any further questions. As Apostle John King Hill always says, "It must be real." Apostle John King Hill concludes that the world could be reached with the Word of God, but it must be by the power of His Spirit. Apostle John King Hill ministers with overwhelming healing, miraculous deliverance, and the prophetic power of God. Apostle John King Hill has prophesied several major world events and personal happenings that were accurate, reliable, and very credible, with others yet to come to pass. Apostle John King Hill has authored several powerful books, including *Power to Overcome the World; The Anointing; Understanding the Anointing; Men of Glory; The Power of Revelation; Beholding the Glory; Glory Dimensions; Dominion Power of Rulership; Mysteries of Heaven; Glory Heaven's Rulership; Breaking the Cycle of Poverty; Spies Among the Church;* and *The Prophets and the Prophetic,* to name a few.

Apostle John King Hill was ordained by the world-renowned servant of God, Rod Parsley, Pastor of World Harvest Church, Columbus, Ohio. Apostle John King Hill holds the following degrees: Bachelor's degree in Biblical Studies, Master's degree in Theology, Doctorate of Divinity, and PhD in Ministry from Canon Bible College and Seminary, Orlando, Florida, USA. Apostle John King Hill is the founder of World Harvesters Outreach Ministries Conferences & Crusades, Inc. Apostle John King Hill is the Host of the Power&Glory World television and radio broadcasts, and has appeared on many Christian Network Televisions around the world: WHT, WHNO 20, The Word Network, Oracle Television Network, The Miracle Channel, Sky Angel, TBN, The Church Channel, Impactv, BellTV, ShawDirect, TelusSatTV, SaskTel Max, TelusOptik TV, and several others. World Harvesters Outreach Ministries Conferences & Crusades, Inc. produces conferences and crusades dedicated to reaching the world with the Word by the power of the Spirit. The call upon this ministry is to reveal God to suffering humanity through the Word of God, and by radical demonstration of His glorious power, until people's heart-troubling questions and circumstances are laid to rest, and they find genuine confidence and good courage to overcome life's obstacles, difficulties, provocations, aggressions, challenges, confrontations, demons, and elements of God's creation.

The goal of this ministry is to reach the world through providing education, leadership training, mentorship, media outreach programs, worldwide evangelistic conferences, and crusades; caring for the needy and less privileged; supporting other organizations of like faith; and showing an example of Christian life.

CONTACT THE AUTHOR

For more information about Apostle (Dr.) John King Hill or to contact the author for worldwide speaking engagements visit:

Website: www.johnkinghillministries.com

Email: jhm@johnkinghillministries.com

Facebook: facebook.com/johnkinghill

Youtube: youtube.com/powerandglorylive

Twitter: twitter.com/powerandglorytv

Or call: 866.978.9324

Additional copies of this book and other book titles from HARVESTERS PUBLISHER™ are available at your local Bookstore.

To view our catalogue online, visit us at:

www.johnkinghillministries.com

Send a request or contact us:

New York, USA

A Division of World Harvesters Outreach Ministries Conferences & Crusades, Inc.

Toll Free: 866.978.9324

media@johnkinghillministries.com

"Publishing the End-Times."

Books by John King Hill

Breaking the Cycle of Poverty

Spies Among the Church

Armor of God

Power to Overcome the World

The Anointing

Dynamic Power of Prayer

Understanding the Anointing

Men of Glory

Power of Revelation

Beholding the Glory

The Glorified Church

Glory Dimensions

Dominion Power of Rulership

Mysteries of Heaven

Mysteries of the Supernatural

Glory Heaven Rulership

Quest for Supernatural

Purpose and Destiny

Men of Purpose

Ultimate Glory Volume 1

Ultimate Glory Volume 2

The Anointing Ultimate Volume Edition

Available from your local bookstore or

www.johnkinghillministries.com

New York, USA

A Division of World Harvesters Outreach Ministries

Conferences & Crusades, Inc.

Give a Gift of Depths

We are always looking to reach every household—around the nation and around the world with the message of the love and power of God through Jesus Christ, whether it relates to salvation, healing, deliverance, prosperity or family!

Join us and be a part.

The Lord gave the word: great was the company of those that published it (Psalms 68:11).

As you share the experience in this book, share it also with someone dear to your heart or even a stranger. Give it as a love gift to as many people as you can, and help us reach millions with the love and power of God!

Use Code 19UPH
For Special Discounted Offer!

Email: offer@johnkinghillministries.com